Negotiation Skills

by Leon Lyons

About the Author

Leon Lyons is a senior coach at Mindset Mastership, a life coaching business based in London, England. Mindset Mastership teaches clients how human behavior really works. Through our teaching we have helped worldwide clients gain a better advantage, to develop themselves and achieve more from life.

WANT A COPY OF MY NEW EBOOK?

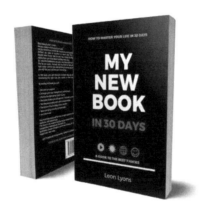

Email me:

MindsetMastership@gmail.com

Table of Contents

Introduction

WHAT IS NEGOTIATION?

Negotiating is not negligible in our day to day activities. Every day we negotiate with our bosses, co-employers or employees, customers, and friends. Even in our homes, we negotiate with our spouses and children. Also, the individuals we sell to and the individuals we buy from. We negotiate prices, products, services, events, schedules, and relationships. Negotiations are not exclusively for wheeler-dealers but also attorneys. It's for everyone, including the regular man or woman!

There are a lot of myths surrounding negotiation. Many estate agents would rather consider themselves as 'negotiators' since they deal with sales, which involves discount or even inflating costs during a property transaction. Many sales representatives associate themselves with the term 'negotiation' or 'negotiator.' What then is 'negotiation' or who's a 'negotiator.' Is it a Dutch auction, starting high and going lower? Another word for selling? These are very popular myths.

Negotiation, in reality, is neither of these. A basic dictionary defines negotiation as 'bargaining or discussing in order to reach an agreement.' Negotiation is a process in which all sides determine the final result. Voluntary consent from both sides involved in a negotiation is required. It is a give and take operation in which the actual terms of a transaction are negotiated. The act or method of negotiation is a process to achieve a mutually satisfactory agreement or target. On both sides, it needs movement, actual or perceived.

Why then do we negotiate? We negotiate basically because we won't get the best offers available to us if we don't. One thing I can guarantee you is that you're already going bankrupt or missing out on the best result if you do not negotiate. The fact is, of course, that many business people do not negotiate; they only make deals with the finest they can, and it affects them every single time.

There are only two pivots in a free market system on which every agreement will eventually be decided: ***price*** and ***value***. The majority of businesspeople rely, incorrectly, on price alone. Focusing on price only will never come with the best offers.

Negotiating is like chess in several respects. In the interest of winning the game, you are willing to sacrifice unique pieces. You know the pieces in chess, but you cannot see into the mind of the other player. You don't know the 'sections' during the negotiation. You have to find and build your pieces and explore ways to understand your counterparts.

UNDERSTAND WHAT NEGOTIATION IS NOT

Negotiations are not the same as sales. The negotiation starts when the sales has been properly made. The easy test is the way the buyer and seller communicate with each other. One individual is persuading in the selling stage, and the other is persuaded. The mindset of both is the same in true negotiation; they both seek to find agreement. The issue is no longer whether or not to make a purchase. The question becomes,' what can I buy or sell, and on what terms? Negotiation assumes that a willingness to buy and a capacity to supply is already developed. The entire focus turns towards the concept of benefit and particular terms or agreements in the negotiation.

When the position of seller shifts to that of negotiator, the sales person sometimes fails to understand, and it costs them. I asked dozens of people for negotiation ideas. The majority of salespeople were struggling to find one. Many of them said,' I do it intuitively.' When I asked them in-depth, the reality was that they did not understand this change from sale to negotiation. As a consequence, they were not successful in each situation.

Negotiation is not 'to give up' or to surrender. A concession may mean submission under the conditions of another person. If we perceive negotiation as surrendering, our thinking will be conditioned, our strategy will be soft, and our dealings will not be effective. That doesn't mean we're not going to step in our talks- we're going to. But we must never give in or step 'one way' in our movement.

It's not a negotiation to dig our heels in. We'll be treated with equal inflexibility if we're been inflexible. Showing our power and trying to look strong does not necessarily mean that the negotiation will be successful. They may represent our confusion and lead to an immediate deadlock, or our counterparts can manipulate them, and benefit greatly from them.

Negotiation is not only about negotiating terms in the buying and selling process; it's about a whole range of problems, such as contested ownership or disputed ownership. There's no chance that you're aware of this. Otherwise, you would not be reading this book. You may have some ideas on what negotiation is, but not the in-depth of the dynamics involved. Instead of putting forward a formal description, let's look at some ideas expressed in negotiation. They are:

1. Negotiation is a way to fulfill your desires, to get what you want or need. We live in a network of relationships and interrelationships and depend on others to support us. Similarly, to better fulfill their own needs, others may approach us. Negotiation is the barter system which streamlines these exchanges.

2. Negotiation is a type of persuasive communication. It's a way to get people to do what we want to do with them. As such, all of our communication skills are required to be used: listening, asking questions, exchanging data, interpreting information, framing ideas, reading facial expressions, influencing and convincing. Empathy and understanding, expertise and perspective, diplomacy, and tact are needed.

3. In relationship with a partner, negotiation is a chance to solve a problem. Unfortunately, bargaining is seen by most people as an opportunity to defeat an enemy, to squeeze much more out of him as feasible. When two or more individuals squeeze simultaneously, however, they aren't likely to get what they want. For any potential partnership, this adversarial strategy also doesn't bode well. When both sides are willing to look at negotiation as a common issue and try to solve it together, both are more likely to fulfill their interests.

Sadly, this is not how many people handle the negotiation, but this book aims to help you shift the attitude and become a win-win negotiator.

4. Negotiation is a tool. Many people like to think of negotiation as a case, where we sit with others at a table, play the negotiation game, try to fulfill our own needs by squeezing or even participating in problem-solving collaboratively. The reality is, talks are beginning earlier than we think. It starts as

soon as we set out to pursue an interest and culminates in an arrangement that completely meets our interests ideally. Do not confuse the grand finale with the job, analysis, and planning that gets us there, the handshake, the signing of the deal.

5. Negotiation is a game. If we take it too seriously, it cannot feel like a game. But it is a game, complete with rules, a game of talent and opportunity. You will decrease the effects of chance if you practice playing a game more skillfully.

6. Negotiating is supposed to be enjoyable, like most activities. A successful, well-played negotiation will leave us feeling happy and rewarded. Joy is in the player's view, and however, with the right mentality, negotiation can be pleasant and satisfying.

WHY NEGOTIATE?

Since we want something we can't get on our own, we negotiate. Someone else is in a role or can help us get it and give it to us. Although somebody might be in a position to hurt our interests, and we try to prevent them from doing so. At this point, we rely on another; we feel helpless, needy, and at the mercy of them. We see another party having jurisdiction over us.

Most times, what we do not see is that our colleague wants something from us as well, or that he's not going to negotiate with us. When he deals with us, we do not see how vulnerable and helpless he feels because he tries not to show it. It's important to note that we are all in a position to have a positive or negative impact on their interests. He's as much in need of us as we are of him.

As a consequence, we find ourselves in a system of interdependencies and relationships. All of us need stuff from everyone else, and we turn to each other for support. Negotiation is the method by which we support each other to get what we need.

POSSIBLE RESULT

There are many potential consequences of any negotiation.

• Win-lose. One side wins, the other loses. This will happen when the parties are not ready or when one party is not ready. It may also be the product of cheating. In any scenario, the loser will blame the winner, and the friendship between the parties will break. Yet, we would just rather win than lose, and it's straightforward to see how this outcome could come in.

• Lose-loss. All sides are struggling. You might be wondering, "Why can it be? It's easy to see how one side could lose, so how do the two parties mutually agree to lose? It's just not fair! "You're right. It's just not rational. It is, though, incredibly quick to get emotional in a negotiation, and one can agree to lose as long as he brings the other person down with him.

• Partial win, partial defeat. Both sides get a part of what they desire, but none have their desires entirely met. This seems logical because both came out happier than they were, and we both realize that we can't possibly hope to get all we want. Or should we do that?

• Win-win. Both sides have everything they want! It is the best of all the world's imaginable. This is the desired result. So while the win-win is much thought about, much sought for, and much prized, it's rarely reached.

WHY SHOULD YOU HAVE TO BE A WIN-WIN NEGOTIATOR

Many experienced people in business have mastered how to negotiate a deal. More often than not, they learned an adversarial, old-school, win-lose negotiation approach. Their teachers became bosses and mentors who learned adversarial negotiation from their former bosses and mentors.

These win-lose negotiators see the negotiation as a cake to be sliced, and each needs a larger one. In other words, one person will win, and the other will lose, so they're going to do their best to win. Since winning and losing is somewhat arbitrary, it becomes obvious that they have won because it is clear that the other has lost. The defeat for the other side is perceived as a victory for them.

This win-lose strategy is only ideal for one-time deals, where you will most likely never see the other party again. You probably don't even care if the other man fails in this case. You may care, however, whether you believe in justice or karma or if you want to preserve a positive image in a world that is becoming smaller and more intertwined by the day. In an isolated situation, though, most individuals just want to succeed.

Yet discrete, one-off talks are the exception. Many of them have to deal repeatedly with the same individuals for a long time, such as bosses, clients, suppliers, and associates. We need to deliver positive outcomes on our side while ensuring a strong, long-term friendship with our negotiation partners. In today's world, a win-win result is quickly becoming the only reasonable outcome.

Only take a look at your computer. Apart from the manufacturer's mark, there are potentially two or three other trademarks added to it, such as Intel or Microsoft. When Intel and the device maker discuss computer chips' cost, do you think any company would embrace a win-lose result? Of course, it's not! They've got to have a win-win contract. I assume that you, too, would prefer to see a win-win deal in most, if not all, of the negotiations. With the tips in this book, the odds of negotiating win-win results will improve exponentially.

THE PROCESS OF NEGOTIATION

I discussed earlier that while the negotiation is generally thought of as an *occurrence*, it is a *procedure*. This method starts when you see a need and set out to fulfill it. You might not even be thinking about negotiating at that stage. You do not know that you are negotiating until you finally agree with others over how much it would cost you to satisfy that need. It's too late—your competitor knows you need him, and he knows you're unprepared.

PREPAREDNESS

In The Art of War, the Chinese military philosopher Sun Tzu wrote, "If you know the foe and know oneself, you don't need to fear the outcome of a hundred battles." In other words, planning is the secret to success in combat. The same could be said of the negotiations.

And how are you preparing for negotiations? Many of the people who are planning to negotiate to buy things will have in mind a very low price that they would love to pay, the best price they can pay, and an amount in the middle of the amount, which is an approximation of what they plan to end up paying. Sellers are going through a similar exercise. It's a smart thing to learn about these aspirations, but it's not enough.

You should conceive of yourself as a big shot negotiator, and you can only do it. But understand this: the only big shot negotiators don't wing it; they're planning. Here are some factors to be kept in mind in your prep work:

• Get to know yourself.

What do you like to do? Not just what you suppose you want, but what you desire. Surprisingly, some people are unaware of this. You might imagine, for example, that you want a wage boost, and maybe you do. But you might like something more, such as respect, to be handled equally, to preserve or boost your quality of life, or to provide protection for your future. A wage increase

• After you've decided what you want—or what you feel you desire.

Get to see that you like it. After telling yourself several times, you might find that, after all, you want something else. You cannot reach a successful result in the agreement until you are transparent about your true priorities and objectives: what you need or want and why you need them.

REGION OF DANGER

Don't say that what you feel you want is going to fulfill your desires. Only remind yourself why you want this to happen. You can find another way to fulfill your needs.

• You will also find that you have many interests.

You need to prioritize these things. For example, when negotiating a job with a new boss, you might be involved in many aspects other than compensation, such as insurance and other incentives, flexible scheduling, work atmosphere, work responsibilities, team assignments, and so on. Some of them are going to be more effective to you than others. It's doubtful you're going to get it all.

Prioritize your wish list to those things that you must have, those that you can compromise with, and those that will be good but not required. Then reflect on your goals to stop disturbing small problems.

• Determine what skills you've got, what you're taking to the table.

What do you even have that your colleague may like to know? These commodities or 'negotiating chips'—anything of worth that you could give for exchange—are called exchange currencies, or merely currencies. How do you rate these currencies to validate your demands?

• What techniques and methods do you use in the negotiating process?

Are you going to make the first bid, or are you waiting for the other side to do so? What sort of sacrifices are you able to make, and when? What's your time? All this is a lot to worry about, but we haven't done it yet! There are also more things you need to consider:

• Get to know the other party.

What exactly does he expect from you? Is he sure about his interests? What are the priorities? Does he just do what he thinks he wants to do, or does he have a secret motive?

• Predict the negotiation approach of your counterpart.

Is he going to be a difficult foe or a collaborating partner? What is his negotiation style, and what tactics will he use?

• Devise a variety of alternatives.

 Based on your knowledge of what you want, the currencies you have, and your understanding of your counterpart's desires, certain options begin to be put together. A potential solution to the negotiating dilemma is an alternative. Build specific solutions that will fulfill your needs as well as those of your counterpart. Be prepared to present and discuss these options.

• Get to know the climate.

You and your counterpart are not going to negotiate in a vacuum. You're both going to be affected by different variables. Some of these you can monitor, others you can expect or respond to. The more you know of them, the higher your odds are.

• Are there any major shifts or patterns in your different industries?

Consider how improvements in interest rates or capital markets can influence your interests. What government laws or legislation could influence you or your counterpart? Will your colleague have a business period that you can know about? E.g., car sales at the ending of the year or toy sales before Christmas could be an opportunity for you.

You can see that there is a lot to be taken into account before you negotiate. To prepare for negotiations, gathering information is important.

BARGAINS

After obtaining facts and planning to negotiate, it must switch to the main event: negotiating. That's what most individuals consider bargaining. This can include face-to-face meetings, phone calls, or e-mail exchanges. You and your counterparts will make proposals and counteroffers, discuss alternatives, verify conclusions, explain understandings, and ideally find an arrangement that suits your respective interests. Just note that the structured meeting case is just part of the negotiation process. The result here depends to a large degree on how much you've trained.

TIMING CONCERNS

Timing problems are an integral aspect of the bargaining process. It might feel like time is against you, but that's because you are painfully conscious of your timelines, revenue goals, and other pressure points. You may be ignorant about what strain your colleague is facing. Understanding a few rules on timing will bring you confidence as a negotiator.

Many individuals appear to overestimate their stresses and vulnerabilities, believing that their counterparts have a better role than they do. Do not think you've had it harder than the other person. They should just keep it cool—wouldn't you?

• If you don't seem to be making a lot of progress quickly in the bargaining phase, try not to worry about it. Continue to negotiate and explore alternatives.

•Know that large holes will be filled in a limited period while the clock goes down.

• You can use time constraints to make improvements. If you are in a state of chaos, try enforcing a time limit to add a safe dose of pressure.

There have been two other points that need to be considered on-time limits:

• Everybody has a deadline, even though you don't know about it.

• A party with the minimum time limitation has the edge over a party with a tight time limitation. If you have a close deadline, I recommend you keep this to yourself. However, please let the other side know that you have a deadline, so it will push them to find an understanding. Apart from time limitations, time management problems need to be considered.

You could be more concentrated in the mornings than in the evening. You may not be in the right mood to bargain on a Monday morning, or you may be overwhelmed by your weekend prospects on a Friday afternoon.

Your business—or your counterpart's—may be subject to a weekly, monthly, seasonal or annual schedule that may impact the negotiating process. Holidays may be a consideration, too. Be mindful of the effect that these time considerations could have on your negotiations.

PLACE AND SEATING

There are few laws and instructions when it comes to location. Until settling on a suitable location that will set the scene for the formal negotiating process, a successful negotiator will weigh any of these variables:

• Where is the negotiation to take place? In your office, or theirs? You may like the feeling of trust and power that comes with the benefit of the home turf, where you can pick the space and the seating arrangements and can influence the atmosphere to project the picture you want. You will require your teammates to back you up and the logistical assistance of your team.

• You would want to meet your counterpart in their location, where they are more relaxed. This offers you the ability to study them on their turf and to make inferences about them. For example, does their company run smoothly, or do they appear to be in disarray? What does the world have to say about their financial situation and their freedom to invest?

• You can prefer to meet on neutral ground, such as a restaurant or a meeting room at the hotel. Meeting on the neutral ground would serve to minimize the benefits of a home-field advantage, which could also draw you away from the stresses of your workplace. Would you prefer a great formal or mediocre informal atmosphere for yourself?

SITTING

There is an explanation of why round tables are used while heads of state gather at an international summit. There is no head of a round table because everybody seems similar. However, most of the business meeting rooms have long tables with a head and a foot. The head is the power seat. It is intended for the leader of the home team, and it adds to his status.

You could be seated at a smaller table. Sitting at a table facing your colleague indicates an adversarial structure. After all, we enjoy chess, table tennis and other friendly games on the opposite side of the table. Sitting side by side, or kitty-corner, implies that both sides, from a shared viewpoint, are solving the dilemma together. This gives a more desirable note. It's much cooler if the table is round. It is still best to recommend seating informally on a couch or benches around a coffee table since this less-daunting casual environment may encourage sharing and might be more pleasant to a candid conversation.

Chapter One:
Leverage Advantages

everage is a term used in various areas, such as economics, mechanics, and negotiation. For example, in bargaining, finance, we hear about leveraged buyouts: the use of credit or debt to finance an acquisition of a corporation, where the company's assets are used as collateral for the loans. People speak about using leverage in mechanics to lift an entity or pry anything loose. Generally, mechanical leverage, such as those that aid teeter-totters or swings, requires a fulcrum. More recently, almost every form of advantage, from leveraging a product's popularity to leveraging consumers, diet, community, political unrest, and much more, has been commonly used to characterize the word leverage.

In the sense of mechanics, one can find the root of the term. Lever, which derives from the Middle English word levour, is the root word for leverage. A levour was a bar used to pry or dislodge something, indicating the means of achieving an aim. One of the advantages of a lever is that it not only helps one to gain an advantage but also to do so at a distance. The distance from the axis (lever) of the direction of a force is often called the leverage of the force, according to the Oxford English Dictionary.

This leverage characteristic, derived from mechanics, can also help us to understand social leverage and how it relates to control. Social leverage and authority are similar even though both include manipulating other parties' actions. However, while control is often more visible, proximate, and permanent (such as the good power that comes from becoming the boss), when it is wielded from a distance, influence is often more subtle and more powerful. The larger the gap, the greater the leverage. In the bible, Goliath had control over David and Goliath (mass, strength), but David overpowered with his slingshot.

LEVERAGE IN ACTION

It is difficult to quantify leverage, similar to other social phenomena, such as love or hate or jealousy. To assess how much love or hatred we have for another, we do not have scales (although we talk about being green with envy, which may be the beginning of a colour-based scale). There is, however, a qualitative measure of social power in a negotiation, measured by the associated costs in failing to achieve an agreement. It is the primary way to grasp leverage, including how to achieve it and modify it. As follows, social leverage is evaluated:

The more it costs Party B to get Party A agreement, the more Party A has control. A famous actress and figure skater named

Sonja Henie made a film called Sun Valley Serenade, directed by Darryl Zanuck in the 1940s. She had an arrangement stipulating that shooting would finish on a certain date. An extra day of shooting was still required when that deadline went away.

But if she was paid $200,000 (an exorbitant amount of money in those days, especially for one day's work), Henie would refuse to complete the film. The studio could'nt afford to cancel the script, having shot almost all of it already. They had to have an arrangement with Sonja Henie, so she had considerable leverage and got the cash.

The pilots of a big airline struggled for better pay many years ago. The union called for wildcat strikes, which means; at the last minute, the pilots would refuse to fly planes. It was difficult to get replacement pilots with just a brief notice. When an airline representative declares that the flight you are about to board would not be operating, after all, imagine your surprise and frustration as a passenger. And then another available flight may or may not exist. Would you like to fly the airline again soon? The risks of not reaching a deal with the pilots' association were immense for the airline. The pilots had control, in other words.

There was one nation from which had easy access, Pakistan, and the United States decided to occupy Afghanistan after the tragedy that occurred September 11. Not only is Pakistan adjacent to Afghanistan, but it offers convenient access for military operations and also provides Al Qaeda forces with possible sanctuary.

The latter could be turned off or reduced at least. The costs of not agreeing with Pakistan were significant for the United States. Therefore, Pakistan had control.

Often, a shared understanding, tradition, or agreement memorializes leverage. There is a general assumption that the sources of journalists would remain confidential. A source could experience professional or personal calamity if that weren't the case. Deep Throat, the nickname that journalists Bob Woodward and Carl Bernstein gave W. Mark, was one of the best examples of this- Label Mark felt their knowledge base for the Watergate scandal.

An investigation by Woodward and Bernstein led to the resignation of President Richard Nixon. Deep Throat would also have been risking electoral suicide by revealing inside information without the guarantee of anonymity. Sources have leverage, however, because any violation of this professional code will likely cause all journalists to dry up as regards information.

As these examples show, the cost of not getting a deal may vary greatly and widely. A price may be financial, as it was for the film studio confronted with not finishing the film starring Sonja Henie. But costs, including time, prestige, face, relationship, culture, psychological well-being, and resources, can take many other forms. As in the airliner scenario whose pilots were striking for decent salaries, there could be many costs at stake. The airline would not only suffer an immediate loss of sales but would also sacrifice any measure of efficiency and goodwill among prospective customers if the pilots' association called a wildcat strike.

Leverage comprehension requires cost comprehension. If there are many costs, then it is important to consider each cost in turn: What is the cost? What is the root thereof? And what is its significance to a group or its relevance? A party sometimes perceives a cost where there is none actually exists, or the costs may change sometimes.

When you want to use leverage and achieve acceptable agreements successfully, it is important to consider the features of costs (and leverage).

FOUR LEVERAGE CHARACTERISTICS

There are four significant features to understand when implementing leverage. The leverage is (1) dependent on expectations, (2) complex, (3) unique to a situation, and (4) social construct.

1. Expectations are based on leverage.

If there is an advantage for a party to an agreement and no one knows that the advantage exists (including the individual with the benefit), there is no leverage. This is particularly true for a faction with a disadvantage. The other side can't exercise an edge if it does not consider the cost of not understanding. Therefore, it is perceived expense, actual or imaginary, that allows leverage.

Consider the example below. To mark your tenth wedding anniversary, you and your partner are planning on spending the weekend in a luxurious honeymoon suite. Your babysitter calls in sick at the last minute. As this is the last major holiday of the summer, nobody else seems to be available.

You contact a nanny you employed many years earlier, who is now in school, as a last-ditch effort. She already has weekend plans; however, you feel you have to try to "buy her out of them." Unknown to you, as you are engaging in this negotiation, your spouse has arranged over the weekend for a friend of the family to take care of your child. If you do not understand the former babysitter, there is no actual cost to you. The former nanny, thus, has control.

In negotiation, perception is everything, and power is dependent on perception. Consequently, despite having enough stock in the backroom, retail stores will often place only one or two of a specific item on a shelf to show that it is common and the store is reduced to its last few. This generates the impression that there are risks involved in delaying your judgment: if you want one of these, buy now because only a few are left.

2. Leverage is flexible.

When new data becomes available, leverage will shift rapidly. For example, if you receive a call from your spouse on your mobile phone while negotiating with the former babysitter, telling you that a family friend will babysit during your anniversary day, your perceived cost of not achieving an agreement will probably decrease dramatically.

In an episode of the sitcom Seinfeld involving the owner of a takeaway food soup establishment, the fickle essence of leverage was most apparent. The proprietor, brilliant yet temperamental, is regarded as the "Soup Nazi."

When ordering soup, customers are supposed to obey a precise schedule or risk getting scolded and barred from the restaurant. Since his soup is out of this universe, everyone obeys his orders. Elaine, however, irritates him on the first visit and gets barred. She tends to end up with the home armoire of the Soup Nazi, which has all his family's soup recipes, through a coincidental chain of events. Elaine is back at his restaurant as the episode finishes, flaunting the ingredients and, in essence, threatening his livelihood. Dramatically, the leverage shifted.

During structured business talks as well, these kinds of adjustments occur. For example, if knowledge central to a forthcoming procurement process known to only one company becomes open to other businesses, then control has shifted among the businesses. Leverage may also alter if one or even more companies' needs or capital backing change, if the negotiating issues are changed (for example, the value of the contract the firms are bidding on is significantly increased), or if newbies join the negotiating process (for example, a new company with deep pockets joins the bidding process).

It is widely agreed that "knowledge is power," which is nowhere more true than leverage management. The life-blood of negotiation is information. The more details you have about the other side's requirements or the availability of various resources or options, the better your negotiating position.

3. Situation-specific leverage is.

The former babysitter had control over the couple looking for a new last-minute substitute in the preceding case. The couple could suddenly have leverage if, though, the nanny required a recommendation for a work application. Likewise, the organization mentioned above with privileged information could have an advantage over the other company. Still, the advantage may be reversed in another case (for example, the second company has just made a technical breakthrough that will revolutionize the industry).

The conditions that produce leverage overlap often, or maybe connected in some way. When asking for a raise, a junior account officer at an advertising agency, recognizing that her job is less than important to the business, may lack leverage. However, if it is required to plan an important ad campaign over the weekends and she is the only one available, then she has control in this case. Besides, in the future, she could try to relate her availability and reliability in securing a raise.

4. A social or relational framework is leverage.

Therefore, one only has an advantage over another person as long as the connection persists. If one party (that is, moves, resigns, separates) leaves the partnership, leverage ceases to exist. This function is noticeable when a husband and wife are divorced and when a son or daughter has become a legal adult and gets out of the home to some degree (gaining scheduling, dietary, and social freedoms). In university environments, the dean's "means of accomplishing an objective" or power easily decreases when a dean steps down and accepts a position alongside the faculty members. Without another band, it's like being by yourself on a seesaw.

THE FOUR LEVERAGE STATES

As power is based on expectations, it is conceivable that a party's benefit can be viewed either, both, or neither side in a negotiation. This provides different degrees of profit. The four states are active leverage, leverage blind, leverage potential, and leverage unknown.

THE ACTIVE LEVERAGE

If the possible costs to the disadvantaged party of not achieving an agreement are understood by both the privileged party in a negotiation and the vulnerable party, the leverage can be characterized as Active Leverage. One clear example of Active leverage is the case of the defective refrigerator me. Active leverage is available from the repairman. He can quickly perceive the costs of not subscribing to his asking price for you (Party B), and you are well conscious of your disadvantage.

BLIND LEVERAGE

It is also necessary, however, to consider the costs involved in not gaining leverage for the disadvantaged group. Peter Sellers played a simpleton called Chauncey Gardiner in the movie "Being There," who have nothing to tell but whose expressions about farming are taken by influential businessmen and politicians as sage metaphors of financial evaluation. Based on the misconceptions of his analytical abilities, Chauncey Gardiner has power or control, even though he is oblivious to this benefit. Similarly, the repairman would have blind leverage if you were to ask a technician to stop by and look at your fridge without knowing the exact nature or severity of your situation.

As these two examples indicate, blind leverage has a degree of efficacy. The other side has power as long as one party perceives that it is at a disadvantage and will incur substantial losses from not achieving an agreement. Occasionally, this occurs in a game of cards, like poker. A more professional poker player may want to fold with a weak hand (for example, a pair of fours) while playing with a beginner since she is unsure her opponent's nonchalance is based on either power or ignorance. The prices could get too high if the bidding persists, so she folds or calls.

However, blind leveraging has its risks. The group with the perceived disadvantage will also test the other party to see if the advantage is known to them. In a poker game, a party with a weak hand might try to bluff, dramatically raising the stakes to indicate to the other faction that it would take a strong position to win. For example, the physician who treated Chauncey for a leg injury was able to determine Chauncey's true degree of intelligence. The Blind Control would have evaporated if he had been able to persuade others that Chauncey's world of practice was restricted to gardening and TV.

Of course, the disadvantaged party may attempt to hide or restrict its expenses. In the event of a malfunctioning freezer, you might decide to ask a neighbour to preserve your frozen meals in their freezer. The repairman does not know the magnitude of your costs if you can only store things there for a day or two, or if you need to get it working quickly because you have relatives coming for a visit.

LEVERAGE POTENTIAL

If the beneficial party perceives its benefit, but the vulnerable party does not perceive the cost of not achieving an agreement, it is possible leverage. He will easily understand the cause and severity of the problem when you call the fridge repairman to explain the issue you are having with your refrigerator. That provides him with potential leverage.

Similarly, when meeting a director or studio executive, a scriptwriter who thinks she has written a successful screenplay has potential power. So does a spouse with two tickets to a sold-out event when he asks his love interest for a date, or an executive of a freight company approaches a potential customer, knowing that a labour strike is about to shut down his chief rival. There was potential leverage for David over Goliath.

Several circumstances could be defined as involving potential leverage. The practice of diplomacy simply means converting possible leverage into active leverage, that is, into a situation in which the disadvantaged party knows the cost of failing to achieve an agreement without creating leverage in the other party's process. This is often done by disclosing details through a third party, while others can find a discreet way for the advantaged party to disclose this information itself or herself. The repairman transfers the leverage from Potential to Active simply by taking your fridge apart and exposing the burned-out coil. He doesn't have anything to say.

Another way in which potential leverage is converted into active leverage is by using sweeteners.

Take, for instance. The salesman offers to throw in a protective coating for the bike while you teeter on a decision about purchasing a new bicycle. To the point of making it irresistible, this item or bid sweetens the deal. The sweetener (an advantage understood by the party making the gesture) constitutes one more cost towards the other party of not achieving an agreement, a downside that until the actual, crucial stage of the negotiation the other side is unaware of. As you are hesitant to determine whether to go ahead with the expensive repair would be a sweetener, the fridge repairman offers a two-year guarantee on materials and labour.

UNKNOWN LEVERAGE

Probably, the condition is not known by either the advantaged party or the disadvantaged party. This is known as undisclosed leverage. Unknown leverage is an unpredictable state, as not achieving an agreement often has perceived costs. Often they naturally emerge, and sometimes one of the parties creates perceived costs. You are with a friend, for instance, who is looking for a new television. You are not in the market for a television, but you happen, to be walking around a TV shop. Multiple work colleagues have these TV's. A sales clerk asks if she could help you. Thanks, you say, but you're just looking. She tells you exactly that they're just on sale today, down 40 percent. Suddenly, the possible cost to you of not reaching a deal is present. Similarly, if the refrigerator engineer could repair other things in the previous example without charging you for another house call, and your waste disposal has recently encountered an occasional issue, this would reflect the repairman's unknown leverage.

Chapter Two:
Manage Emotions On Both Sides

Emotion in any human interaction, including negotiation, is always present. Both of us have them, but we've got to deal with them, ours and theirs. They can't be ignored because they affect all of us. The way we think, feel and behave is influenced by emotions. The only thing to do is consider them and constructively deal with them. Some feelings are positive: satisfaction, trust, fun. Others are negative: annoyance, fright, humiliation. Negative emotions, which contribute to a win-lose dynamic, tend to trigger competitive impulses. Positive emotions foster teamwork and promote win-win results.

Often, feelings are infectious. We may disperse them to others and capture them. Generally speaking, the individual who communicates her feelings more strongly will affect the less articulate person.

The results are clear for negotiation. In herself, a win-win negotiator can handle the negative feelings and not worsen them in others. She can also exhibit positive feelings and will say and do things that in others are likely to bring out positive feelings. Sounds easy enough, doesn't it? Sadly, it's not simple— not even for Freud!

THE EMOTION LANGUAGE

Many individuals think of negotiation as a contest. Win-win negotiators think of it as a chance to work together to address a common issue. This mindset can help or detract from the language you use, so that's why choosing your words wisely is essential.

Words like 'I,' 'me,' 'my,' 'mine,' 'you,' 'your,' and 'your' foster competitive negotiation dynamism. 'I' and 'you' clearly contrast and make it very clear that we are at the spectrums' opposite ends. These terms suggest that I am going to win and you are going to lose, or you are going to win and I am going to lose. A win-win result with a 'me versus you' mindset is difficult to achieve. There may be moments when you need to say 'I' or 'you,' but if possible, try and avoid these words. Try to use 'we', 'us', and 'our' instead.

These terms reflect teamwork and indicate that we are all working together on the same side to solve our problems. The use of 'we' and other collaborative languages helps to set the winning tone.

If it does come down to 'I' or 'you,' though, an 'I' statement works much well than a 'you.' For instance:

"Too high is your initial offer."

This sounds judgmental, dressed up as reality with an opinion. An implicit critique is also present, which will place the other side on the defensive. In an aggressive dynamic, he can react by holding on to his stance more tightly and attempting to justify it. Instead, consider this:

"Your initial offer is too high, I feel."

That's my view here. It's the way I do. We're all entitled to thoughts and views of our own. It's even better if I can provide a supporting explanation. It is non-judgmental in any situation. Without any bad feelings, we will continue the talks.

These examples emphasize emotions and expectations, in addition to using 'I' rather than 'you.' You may not share your thoughts or perceptions with your counterpart, but he can hardly blame you for them. Any more instructions to consider are here:

AVOID USING EXPRESSIONS THAT SAY THE OTHER PERSON IS TO BLAME OR IS INCORRECT.

Do not criticize, judge or blame yourself. This will put your counterparts on the defensive only. Emphasize your thoughts and perceptions instead.

Consider, for instance:

Don't make me rush! "

This indicates that I am being pressured unfairly by the other side. It means I am judging him. He might hate the inference.

"I would like to think about it for some time."

Without regard to the motifs of the other party, this reflects my feelings.

It is unable to offend.

Describe instead of judge. Describe It is possible to refute an accurate description of reality, but its very nature will not offend the way a decision will.

For instance:

"Your offer is disproportionately low."

With this decision on your side, your counterpart may be offended. You say that he is irrational.

"In light of current market trends, I feel your offer of a three percent increase is inadequate."

This declaration, even if "current industry trends" are debatable, is more precise, descriptive, and verifiable. It is non-judgmental and unlikely to incite crime.

The terms we use in a negotiation have a huge impact on their emotional environment.

Ignore derogatory words, value-laden words and words that are emotional or hotkey—using terms that are optimistic, collaborative and supportive.

In negotiation, typical emotions are encountered by people, most of which do not affect the negotiation. Rage and anxiety are the two ones most likely to disrupt a negotiation.

INFURIATION

It is commonly believed that anger is an ugly emotion, a monster that appears in stressful circumstances to enable us to bully, punish and take revenge. The most challenging emotion to manage is anger. Although it can seem acceptable to express frustration at the moment, it is rarely retrospective, and we generally regret it afterwards. There is a different way to look at frustration, however. This helps to shield us from any perceived danger to our well-being or self-esteem.

To cause the other party to fear, we also show frustration, thereby granting us some leverage over them. When we are desperate to win, having our way, or justifying ourselves to be 'right,' this is simple to understand. Strong and in charge, we must appear. Rage lets this be done to us.

As anger is a defensive emotion, we must question what we are defending ourselves from when we feel anger. A danger we experience. What hazard is there? Similarly, we have to note when we see another person showing frustration because he feels threatened. What is it that scares him? What is he trying to safeguard?

The rule is: don't show your annoyance. There are exceptions, of course.

If you show anger, do so because, when justified, you want to act angry. A hard-nosed negotiator, for instance, can threaten you to test your answer. Although the best response is usually to stay calm and in charge, you may decide that a managed release of anger or a showing of moral outrage can show your counterpart that you are not a coward. Mar Tough Guy could view this as a show of power, and I admire you more for it. He won't mess with you again, having proven your mettle.

In hopes of gaining a concession from you, some negotiators will generate an explosion of rage. However, without resorting to such low strategies, win-win negotiators are capable of generating value.

Suppose a win-win negotiator is not your counterpart. Suppose he's not able to control his thoughts or use his rage as a club. How do you react?

My ideas are here:

You have to allow his frustration to run its course, first of all. In an emotion-driven state, you can't reason with others, so don't even try. Stop this debate. Yeah, let him vent. This would be a great time for a break.

Only after his rage has dissipated does he continue bargaining. Just because an individual has cooled down, do not presume that he is no longer upset. Chances are, the emotions underlying the irritation are still there. These concerns you have to answer, but only after the psychological storm has ended.

Accept as real his frustration. Your counterpart has a right to his emotions through voicing anger is not always acceptable.

You could say:

"You're angry, I see. You have a deep feeling about this, and I want to understand why it is important to you.

Encourage him, and listen carefully to share his thoughts.

In the face of an outburst of anger from your colleague, retain your calm. Don't fight fire with fire; you're just going to get a larger fire!

Do not personally take it. Your counterpart may be dissatisfied with the situation, upset with himself, or trying to hide his vulnerability or insecurity. Do not presume that you are the mark because you're not likely to be.

By making a concession, do not please your counterpart. Just offer a concession in return for your counterpart's concession, and only at a point when justification prevails. When you give something up to buy the other party's approval, guess what you'll get? Further outbursts! Your counterpart would have found a good strategy for bargaining with you, and why not?

Apologize if warranted, or even if it isn't. Nothing costs an apology, and it makes the other person feel better. Don't let pride come in the way of your desires being fulfilled. Concentrate on the big picture.

FEAR

There are four fundamental forms of fear: fear of the unknown, fear of defeat, fear of failure, and fear of rejection. They all have consequences for negotiators, so you should understand and be prepared to deal with how they affect you and your counterpart.

FEAR OF THE UNKNOWN

People are afraid of what they do not know or understand. There may be high stakes and unpredictable results in a negotiation; the process may be unknown, thus instill fear.

Preparation is the solution to this. Know as much about your preferences and currencies as possible, as well as your counterpart's interests. Develop a strong Plan B. Collect knowledge on the subject matter and the negotiating context. Preparation contributes to trust, and trust helps you control fear.

FEAR OF LOSING

No one likes to lose, but there is a clear aversion to risk among some people. Most individuals are more motivated mainly by a fear of failure than by the prospect of profit. Their fear of losing cash or paying too much can lead them to miss a good chance. Instead, their fear of losing out on a chance might lead them to make a bad deal.

Preparation tends to overcome the fear of failure as well. Know your bottom line and your Plan B before you begin negotiating, and stick to them. Be able to walk away. In the light of new knowledge and changing circumstances, you should reassess these but do so with the very same sobriety that went into your initial pre-negotiation evaluation.

Furthermore, consider that calculated risk isn't just about a foolish risk. In a negotiation, there will always be some element of risk. If you enable yourself to overcome fear, you won't negotiate a lot, nor will you learn a lot. Know that there are elements of talent and opportunity in negotiation and the more experienced you are in planning, the less chance affects you.

FEAR OF FAILURE

Fear of failure and fear of loss always go hand in hand. Fear of loss is tangible (money, chance), while fear of failure is an intangible loss, such as harm to confidence, ego, credibility, humiliation or loss of face. It can be more difficult to absorb these emotional losses than monetary losses.

A negotiator will disregard his best interests and join a lost cause because of the very possibility of losing face. Since he doesn't want to admit that he was wrong, in the irrational expectation that things will turn out better, he decides to follow a doomed plan. And experienced negotiators are struck by this escalation of dedication. Guard against it with detailed planning for pre-negotiation and asking team members during the negotiation for fact checks.

As well as fear of losing and fear of the unknown, a win-win mentality will offset the fear of failure. Approaching a negotiation as an opportunity to solve a dilemma with your partner collaboratively minimizes the fear of failing or losing, as both sides concentrate on achieving a win. The emphasis on asking questions, hearing and empathizing generates trust and sheds some light on the unknown. As anxiety takes a back seat, the spirit of pursuing alternatives and building meaning keeps the conversation optimistic.

FEAR OF BEING REJECTED

Fear of rejection is a special type of fear of failure. We do not want to hear the word "no." Most people get frustrated and give up after hearing the word "no." They equate rejection of their proposal to a personal rejection of them. For fear that they will be seen as overbearing, they are scared to pursue the matter. They just don't want to risk more rejection sometimes.

Reassure yourself that only your idea is being dismissed for resolving this fear of rejection, possibly because your counterpart does not understand your request. "Continue with a "Why not? To understand her reasoning. Make sure she understands you.

The word 'no' is never final. Treat it as an opening place if you hear a "no." Modify and suggest other choices for your proposal. Try converting this "no" into a "yes."

Preparation, a major theme that I have stressed in this book, is the secret to overcoming these fears. Furthermore, note these tips:

Do not seem too eager for an agreement. Your partner will be able to negotiate with you on his terms until you show an emotional desire for the negotiation issue.

Have a good Plan B. This makes you confident and ensures that you will not be worse off than before after the agreement.

Be poised to walk away. It is worse to make a bad deal than to make no deal at all.

Bear in mind that, to a degree, your negotiating partner, being human, also experiences these worries. How much depends on his values, level of trust, readiness and strength of will.

MANAGING STANDARDS, MAKING THEM SATISFIED

A major part of the negotiation is understanding. The thing that matters is not whether you win or lose. It is whether you know you have won or lost. More significant than any objective indicator of the outcome is the subjective result. People, regardless of how well they do, ought to feel positive about the process and the result.

As such, we saw that haggling and feigning hesitation is better than accepting the first bid. We got to play the game. We've got goals to fulfill.

The negotiating process must, however, tend to be fair. We have a clear sense of equity that is hard-wired into our minds. Your counterpart will despise you, and your partnership will suffer if you or the method seems unfair.

The argument is demonstrated by an occurrence common in negotiation classes. Students were paired up, and each student was given $1000 to share with his partner. The partners, however, have the option to accept the offer and share or reject the money, in which situation no one gets any cash. Invariably, a 50:50 bid is accepted. The first student also feels entitled to a greater share and proposes a split of 60:40 or a split of 75:25. Some of these would be accepted, but the more unfair the split offered, the more likely the spoiler will be played by the second student and refuse the bid. A reasonable person would consider even a $10 bid, as he'd be monetarily better off.

But individuals are not logical; they are emotional, and they have a good sense of equity. They can choose a lose-lose option.

BIASES

And the way we allocate credit and blame, we appear to have those prejudices. We are likely to experience the outcome of our abilities when things work out positively for us. "I have achieved a good result because I have worked hard, I have prepared, I am a great negotiator, and I merit it." We find external explanations to justify the results when we don't do so well. They were lucky, they were deceiving me because the economy was working against me, and there was nothing.

I might do that. Instead, we can discount the impact of situational variables and conclude that our counterpart has more talent, experience or skill than he does.

A win-win negotiator aims to be open to options and be objective. She's always going to be prejudiced, but she's going to be more prepared to admit that she has flaws and makes mistakes. You have a chance to learn from your failures and do better next time when you accept responsibility for your shortcomings. We also like to assume that things are going to work out better for us than others. "That can never happen to me; it only happens to other people." Some people say that in life, they only get lemons, and everyone else has better.

We also think about ourselves more favorably than others. I am smarter, more professional, more trustworthy, more open-minded, and more righteous than him. He is so rigid, unreasonable, and biased." You probably think the same thing about your counterpart!"

A win-win negotiator understands that both she and her counterpart have these prejudices. She strives to recognize as equal to the other party.

She acknowledges that their confidence and communication will suffer from thinking poorly of her counterpart, as will the possibility of achieving a win-win outcome.

Chapter Three:
Identify Opportunities

Most of the time, because existing businesses successfully satisfy consumer needs, the world does not require new companies. There is no incentive for entrepreneurs to build viable new ventures as a result. Sadly, in the absence of business opportunities, many entrepreneurs do not know this and build new companies. In a short period, these new companies collapse. To be effective, in response to an opportunity to develop a new product or service that meets consumer needs that have not been adequately met or that serves customer needs in a far better way than existing businesses meet them, you need to start your new company. So, where are these possibilities coming from? What type are they taking? How can successful entrepreneurs balance creativity with opportunities? How do these opportunities define successful entrepreneurs? These questions are answered in this chapter.

SUPPLIERS OF OPPORTUNITIES

Entrepreneurial possibilities are circumstances in which an entity has an opportunity to launch a product that produces more revenue than it costs to manufacture. Such cases arise when the needs of consumers are not met or when it is possible to address those needs in a different way than is currently being done. So, why are there these opportunities? After all, if the possibilities are valuable, why have they not already been used by someone else? One explanation is that there has just been some kind of shift to open up an opportunity to try something different or do something in a better way. Take, for instance, the chance to record music on disk drives. Before the advent of the laser made it possible, this potential did not exist. The connection between change and the development of opportunity suggests that recognizing the change that makes the opportunity feasible is the first step in determining a valuable opportunity. In general, there are four types of changes that generate opportunities for new businesses: technological changes, changes in political and regulatory laws, changes in demographic factors, and changes in the structure of an industry. Successful entrepreneurs understand how each of these sources creates a shift that makes entrepreneurial opportunities feasible.

SHIFT IN TECHNOLOGY

As you imagine, technological progress is one of the most significant triggers for launching new high-tech enterprises, primarily because technological change enables individuals to do something that could not be done before or could only be done less efficiently. Take, for example, the development of the computer program behind e-mail. This program made it possible to connect in ways that are more effective than the phone, fax, or letters, and thus opened up an important opportunity. So, what are the characteristics of technological transition associated with developing new industries with valuable opportunities? The size of the technological shift is important. The greater the technological transition, the greater the potential to build new industries as greater changes in magnitude impact more technology uses, enabling more products to be used by new technology. Take, for example, the creation of a new form of an electrical circuit. If the new circuit is just 10 percent faster than the older one, only a small number of items can replace the older circuit. The new circuit would only be used for those goods where a 10 percent increase will surpass the adjustment cost.

In comparison, if the new circuit is 500 percent faster than that of the older one, in a much wider variety of things, its advantages would outweigh the cost of the upgrade. Then the generality of the shift is there.

Some technologies are general-purpose technologies, including the laser. They contribute to the development of a wide variety of new goods. The laser, for example, has made new items such as supermarket scanners, medical equipment, and CD / DVD players possible. Since general-purpose technologies can be implemented in various fields, they open up more possibilities than single-purpose technologies for new products and services. The commercial feasibility of the move is also there. Some emerging technologies have a large-scale impact but do not produce much commercial profit directly. The space shuttle, for example, is a very big shift over choices for going into space because it saves a massive amount of money on missiles that cannot be reused. The commercial advantages of the space shuttle, however, are very limited because there are only a few applications that can be installed on it. Finally, the impact of technological transition on the dynamics of the industry is present. One reason why technological disruption is also a big source of opportunity for new companies to start is that it changes the way companies compete with each other. Take the impact of telecommunications in the telephone industry, for example. This technology has transformed a capital-intensive company into one needing little capital. As a result, it generates opportunities for new companies that are at a disadvantage in sectors that are capital intensive.

SHIFT IN POLITICS AND REGULATION

Political and regulatory reform is another form of change that opens up possibilities for new companies. This form of transition creates possibilities because it improves productivity. For example, telecommunications deregulation has encouraged many new companies to form and implement less costly forms of transmitting voice and data that have benefited both businesses and consumers. In other instances, the incentive created by political and regulatory changes is not positive but merely transfers value from one collection of economic factors to another. For example, a city ordinance requiring anyone to use two grounding rods for electricity will provide an incentive for a business person to take wealth away from customers, even with one grounding rod. Since there is no particular advantage to the grounding rod, the ordinance provides an incentive that is not productive but rather transfers' capital. Why do changes in politics and legislation boost entrepreneurship opportunities? Deregulation generates opportunity because it encourages entrepreneurs who would have been barred from entry under a controlled system to bring forward more ideas. Deregulation often removes many of the hurdles and regulatory barriers to the formation of new companies. Many entrepreneurs do not build new companies because, under controlled regimes, these activity costs become too high. When deregulation happens in ways that haven't been lucrative before, entrepreneurs see company creation as profitable. Unique regulations also make feasible activities to be sponsored by such regulations by growing demand for them. Legislation mandating the use of car seats, for example, raises the demand for them and opens up opportunities for producing and selling car seats. To promote those practices, certain political and regulatory reforms give incentives or other tools, lowering certain development costs by making them more popular. For instance, University of Toronto economist Maryann Feldman found that the procurement policies of the U.S. government made it possible for novel technological companies to be established in the area of Washington, D.C. By taking advantage of the new rules for the procurement of IT services by the federal government, several new companies have been able to find a niche for their services then get off the ground.

SHIFT IN SOCIAL AND DEMOGRAPHIC AFFAIRS

Social and demographic change is another major type of change that creates business opportunities. By altering people's tastes and generating demand for products where demand had not existed before, societal and demographic developments open up opportunities for digital technology companies. The demographic shift of women joining the workforce, for example, and the resulting rise in demand for speed in food processing, allowed them to sell many frozen foods. A social trend is one significant kind of demographic and social change that generates opportunities. The chance to manufacture deodorant, for instance, was the consequence of a societal trend that led the majority of people to conclude that body odour was disgusting. Although there is currently no medical or health need for individuals to mask body odour, the social development movement assumes that body odour is nasty has made it possible to manufacture goods that mask that odour. Another significant kind of shift that contributes to the development of entrepreneurial opportunities is demographic changes. The U.S. population is ageing, for instance, as birth rates decrease and people live longer. This demographic change makes it possible to implement goods and services, such as those in senior medical services, for which adequate demand didn't exist 25 years ago. Yet, a shift in understanding or demand is another form of social or demographic change. Sometimes, individuals decide that they want something different or view things in a new way. The view of the American flag just after the events of September 11 is a good instance of this form of transition. The demand for the American flag has risen significantly, primarily due to shifts in the American public's views of what the flag symbolizes. Many improvements incorporate both social and technical variables. Companies such as Net Babysitter and Cyber Patrol, for instance, have taken advantage of an opportunity to shield kids from harmful Internet content. This potential emerged both because of the Internet's technological growth and the social trend of kids being home alone after class.

CHANGES IN THE STRUCTURE OF INDUSTRY

Changing the structure of the sector is another form of shift that is a source of business ventures. Often, the business structure changes when businesses that supply other companies or major clients die or because companies combine or acquire each other. These types of changes alter an industry's competitive dynamics and open up or close down niches that can provide entrepreneurs with opportunities. For example, as the aviation industry consolidated based on the hub and spoke design used by major airlines, opportunities started to occur for entrepreneurs to join and build new airlines flying point-to-point. The transition to the hub and spoken approach alone was not enough to create an opportunity for new companies to enter; this business opportunity was created by combining the aviation industry's change combined with the company exit.

ACKNOWLEDGING A PRECIOUS OPPORTUNITY

Knowing that an opportunity exists is the next step in the process of finding a valuable opportunity. People also realize with retrospect that a very reasonable possibility for a new technology company that someone else has abused has been overlooked. So, why do certain individuals find useful resources and not others? To address this question, it is important to note that there are entrepreneurial opportunities due to changes in knowledge about technological change, the nature of the market, social and demographic developments, and changes in policy and regulations. It is fair that access to data or the ability to process it is the secret to what makes it possible to identify opportunities. Certain individuals, for example, are the first to hear about a technical discovery, possibly because they work in a research laboratory where innovation is made. Accessing this data before others can think about it helps individuals to make better choices about producing and selling new products than others.

ACCESS TO FACTS

Some individuals have greater access to data about the developments that open up entrepreneurial possibilities than others. Several factors tend to be very important, and successful entrepreneurs use these factors to recognize lucrative opportunities. Many individuals have stronger positions on social networks. Being well placed in a social network enables a person to gain access to that information that cannot be accessed by others because the information is also shared via the social connections of people. Friends and associates also tell you stuff you will not discover in other ways, such as the fact that in a few months, a storefront will become empty or that new technology has been invented. If you have the right contacts and others do not, you can gain access to information that cannot be accessed by other people. Besides, strong social relations facilitate the transfer of data from one individual to another by getting people more likely to trust in the transfer of information under uncertain conditions. People find it hard to know if the information they hear is correct. Is a recent technological discovery, such as cold fusion, for instance, true or a hoax? Most individuals rely on their buddies and trusted people to figure out just what information to believe to determine whether evidence is reliable. Therefore, individuals with close social links to knowledge outlets regarding key changes that serve as sources of opportunity will sometimes have access to that information, while other individuals cannot. Some individuals have employment or life activities that bring them closer to the source of knowledge about the developments that create new opportunities. Jobs in research and innovation and marketing tend to be especially useful for creating high-technology companies to provide access to knowledge on developments that open up opportunities.

Innovation jobs provide information on newly-emerging innovations that generate opportunities for new enterprises. Marketing jobs provide consumer desires, or unfulfilled customer needs with details. As a result, these positions are very useful in placing people in the flow of data to learn about the possibilities for new businesses to be found. This is not to suggest that other occupations do not have access to knowledge about prospects for entrepreneurship. While marketing and innovation provide, on average, access to more of that information, sufficient information ultimately depends on the level of the opportunity. For example, since they work in a company's finance unit, not marketing or research and development, an accountant might know about the opportunity to develop a company to provide accounting software. On average, however, innovation and marketing workers have greater access than other jobs to knowledge about potential entrepreneurs. Some individuals also have access to data that others do not have about the adjustments that create opportunities because they are searching for that data. Although random searching will not help you gain access to knowledge that generates opportunities, focused efforts may provide useful information about the origin of the opportunity to find a solution to technological or business problems. Biotechnology researchers at several universities, for example, are actively looking for cancer remedies. They know that discovering a cancer cure would allow them to start a business to take advantage of that cure. They try, in essence, for the root of entrepreneurial potential.

BETTER COLLECTION OF INFORMATION

Access to knowledge is just part of understanding why certain individuals and not others find prospects for new companies. Another important part is that from bits of knowledge about the developments that make new companies possible, they are better able to develop new business ideas. It's not trivial, this part. Just because you know that new technology doesn't mean you're going to think of a company to exploit it. Take the Swiss jewelers who invented the smartwatch technology, for instance. Since these jewelers couldn't figure out how to produce watches using this technology, they gave the technology effectively to Japanese companies, who found out how to sell it. Several aspects of the mental capacities of people impact the processing of knowledge and help them recognize business opportunities. Some individuals have mental schemes about markets and ways to serve them that help them understand and use data in ways that other individuals do not.

Knowledge leading to identifying a business venture does not exist in the way of a ready-to-introduce prepackaged product or service. Rather, given the new technology, fresh legislation, new market structure, or new demographic pattern, it comes as a hint or signal that something might be done to build a new enterprise. Therefore, a mental method involving extrapolating from bits and pieces of information is detecting good growth opportunities.

Chapter Four:
Exploiting Weakness

We have a huge advantage as creative practitioners when communicating and negotiating with anyone. We are profoundly in contact with our feelings, and we have instincts that are finely tuned that give us a unique ability to interpret others' emotions. This is why, after all, people employ us: to evoke emotion and drive people to action.

Sadly, these characteristics are frequently viewed as undesirable in a company. We are advised that it makes us look fragile or insecure by expressing emotion.

In my experience, however, tuning and weakness are naturally derived abilities that benefit us. In a meeting, paying enough attention to the unspoken dynamics allows us to read intent and anticipate how others will behave, just like a chessboard is read by a grandmaster. Listening to our intuition and understanding when and how to act is essential.

It is a means of deepening human experiences to expose our true selves, including our vulnerabilities. A vulnerability or insecurity, you share a description of your true self, and your new friend also shares this about herself. That's part of what strengthens our bonds and helps us feel closer.

I've learned over the years that, when bargaining, we should use the same tactics. Confidence exchanged will deepen the business relationships in this manner. And can also put into the picture an additional sense of collaboration and empathy. Your client is not an enemy now, but someone on your side, or even cheering for you.

Of course, be mindful of the environment. In intimate relationships or family dramas, a client's meeting isn't the time to reveal the weaknesses. This is about highlighting the weakness of your bargaining stance.

To deepen consumer relationships and encourage empathy in others, here's how to use weakness:

- ADMIT TO NERVOUSNESS.

"I have never addressed a lot of people like that before, so please endure with me. Maybe I'm not at the top of my game."

- DISCLOSE YOUR INSECURITY.

I know you have a lot more experience with this than I do, Diane, so can I rely on your assistance to get through it, please? "

- SHARE YOUR PASSION.

This is such a dream idea for me, Bob, you know. I'd love to be involved so much, and I know I'd do a great job.

Research indicates that those feelings move more easily when you accept feelings of distress than if you ignore them. So it helps you stay relaxed by exposing your weakness, and it encourages compassion from your clients or business associates.

But what if you are around people who are not empathetic? Or are you in a corporate structure where pressure is so entrenched that the slightest indication of weakness is eagerly taken advantage of by co-workers? In these situations, it may be a liability instead of a strength to disclose too much. They go for the jugular when these individuals smell blood. With caution, it is essential to try.

And how are you able to tell the difference? Checking what others say is one way. Former partners, customers, and friends are also prepared to share their interactions with a specific organization or individual. Plus, here's where you get our sophisticated intuition. We can discern profound truths about people several times by actually tuning in to our intestinal reactions. By asking detailed questions about the individual, you are working with, set up small tests. And pay your close observations attention.

Here are a couple of questions that might help:

Does it seem authentic or fake to John?

Do you know that you can trust him? Did he have you undermined?

Did he abide by his contracts with you?

In his relations with you, is he just looking out for himself?

We sometimes interpret a lot through our intuition about others, but then we miss our conclusions. This, my experience reveals, is never wise.

And there's a lot of research that reinforces the value of trusting your intuition. Listen to your intuition, and then use vulnerability as a strength to build understanding and empathy if it's safe to show yourself.

In your negotiating skillset, your instincts are a strong and strategic weapon. Use them now!

TIPS FOR NEGOTIATING FROM A POSITION OF WEAKNESS.

Their techniques recommended include the following:

• DO NOT DISCLOSE THAT YOU ARE WEAK

It is not troublesome to have a weak BATNA (Best Alternative to a Negotiated) if the other side does not realize that your BATNA is weak. Do not advertise it if you have a bad BATNA!

• OVERCOME YOUR VULNERABILITY BY EXPLOITING THEIR WEAKNESS

If both sides have a poor BATNA, this means that the possible agreement zone is wide. In other words, when the two parties reach an agreement, a lot of value is generated. Who does more of this value claim? The one who does best is the one who in the negotiation makes the vulnerability on the other side more salient.

• IDENTIFY YOUR UNIQUE VALUE PROPOSITION AND EXPLOIT IT

Quite often, you bring something that differentiates you from your rivals to the table. This is your Separate Value Proposal (SVP), and it does not have to be a lower price. You could have a better product, a higher-quality service, a powerful name, a good reputation, or a host of other assets that you're negotiating partner values and that you can offer more efficiently or cheaper than your rivals.

- TAKE INTO ACCOUNT RELINQUISHING WHAT LITTLE CONTROL YOU HAVE IF YOUR POSITION IS VERY POOR.

You may want to avoid flexing your muscle and, rather, simply ask them to help you if you can't outsmart the other party in a negotiation. Others reciprocate when negotiators attempt to exploit their strength. Because you're on the weaker side, this trend can be catastrophic. But when you clarify that you have no intentions of actively fighting or bargaining, others will soften their stance as well.

- STRATEGIZING BASED ON THE WHOLE PORTFOLIO OF NEGOTIATIONS

When implementing your negotiating plan, audit the false beliefs you make. If you just quantify strength as the ability to press hard in any provided negotiation against losing the contract, you may view yourself as 'weak.' But you can find that once you start thinking about your capacity to endure losing some deals, you are very "strong" because you are optimizing the quality of your overall portfolio of negotiations.

- GROWING YOUR POWER BY BUILDING COALITIONS WITH MANY OTHER WEAK PARTIES

In the field of international affairs, and during 2003 WTO negotiations in Cancun, Mexico, a vivid illustration of the strength of coalitions appeared. It was disgruntled at the persistent lack of attention paid to developed nations' issues of concern. Twenty-one "weak" nations joined forces to form the Party of 21. This coalition is now in a far better position than any member nation could be on its own to bargain for its members' rights.

- USE YOUR EXTREME WEAKNESS' POWER-THEY WILL NEED YOU TO SURVIVE

"If you bully me too hard, you'll wreck me — and risk a value-creating partner.

- UNDERSTAND — AND STRIKE — THE SOURCE OF THEIR STRENGTH

An especially innovative tactic for fighting back against protesters collectively referred to as the "Pledge-a-Picket" Initiative, has been embraced by several Family Planning clinics across the nation. Here's how it works: The clinic asks its advocates on a per protester basis to commit donations to the clinic. The more demonstrators turn up to pick up the clinic, the more donations the clinic generates funds! Even outside its clinic, the Family Planning of Central Texas in Waco has posted a sign reading: "Even Our Protesters Embrace Family Planning."

When the clinics of Planned Parenthood realized that the root of their critics' strength was the ability to attract large numbers of demonstrators outside the facility, they could think of a creative way to minimize the advantages of doing so.

Chapter Five:
Building Immediate Rapport

Rapport implies putting another individual at ease and having a real bond. From the start, you must strive for this right. Be friendly, respectful, and welcoming. Have small talks. You are using the name of the individual. Yeah. Smile. Offer him a beverage or do him a little favour. Set a pleasant tone and create a dynamic of collaborative working.

Similarity and harmony are the core of rapport. Their sound, speed, rhythm, volume and several features of their body language will be identical when two individuals are truly in touch. This will occur naturally, but by deliberately mirroring elements of the vocal tone and body language of your counterpart, you will facilitate the process. Sit if he is seated, and stand if he is standing. Position yourself at his height. To build a sense of similarity, use body language far beyond basic eye contact, grin and handshake.

By implementing key vocabulary as the other person, you can also underline similarity and promote the relationship. Use them yourself if she tends to use those terms. She's going to note, maybe subconsciously, that there is something she likes about you. People want individuals who are like them to be like the individual with whom you are.

EMPATHIZING

The famous psychologist Carl Rogers interpreted empathy as entering the world of another person non-judgmentally. You can fully comprehend him when you enter his world freely and see it as he sees it. There's no reason for you to agree with him. Just strive to consider his point of view.

There is a saying by lawyers that an agreement is a mutual understanding. If you and I do have the same idea in mind, in other words, then we agree. Imagine that we were not only willing to have a meeting of minds but also a meeting of hearts. If you can comprehend what I think and also feel what I feel, that is empathy!

QUESTIONS

Asking questions helps you to establish relationships, collect knowledge, and confirm understanding, and monitor the negotiation's speed and direction. Ask questions, and listen to the replies.

LISTENING

Let much of the talking be done by your counterpart. The more he speaks, the more details you hear. You know what you think already—wouldn't it be nice to know what your counterpart appears to think? Listening also reveals that you value him and that his viewpoints concern you.

PAY CLOSE ATTENTION TO TALKING NON-VERBALLY

It is always more important to have non-verbal communication than words alone. Is your counterpart accessible and available, or protective and secretive? Is he honest or misleading? Is he willing, desperate, confused, interested? Learn how to read the facial expressions and body language of your counterpart.

A double-way street is a non-verbal contact. Be mindful of the nonverbal messages that you send to others. Drumming on the table with your fingers might indicate that you are nervous or impatient. Arms crossed around your chest may indicate that you are uncomfortable or protective. The lack of eye contact shows a lack of trust. Avoid facial expressions and body language, which convey poor or negative qualities. Use body language that shows the attributes you want to project: trust, competence, preparation and professionalism. Make sure to keep your halo gleaming and polished.

GROW TRUST

Trust is the pillar of any successful negotiating partnership. In less time and with less formality, negotiators who have a confident partnership can conclude better agreements. They are less likely to have conflicts, and when they do occur, they are more likely to settle the disputes amicably.

By actually meeting your counterpart as a person, you can develop a confident relationship. Spend time socializing and informally getting to know one another. This getting acquainted approach is important in certain societies, and they will not get back to work until they feel relaxed with their counterparts.

It is not sufficient to get to know each other socially. Often, you must be trustworthy. You must gain the trust of another person and merit it. To improve your trustworthiness, here are some ways:

- BE TRUTHFUL.

Keep your word and uphold a reputation for truthfulness.

- BE TRANSPARENT.

Being transparent and above board would make it possible for others to trust you. You don't have to say anything to them; it is perfectly sufficient to tell your counterparts that such information is confidential.

- BE COHERENT.

Individuals are more at home with others that have set principles explicitly and adopt them without fail. Under-promise still and over-deliver.

- RESPECT THE COLLABORATION.

In a relationship with a trusted individual, the partnership's potential is more essential than every negotiation result. Make sure your counterpart understands how you feel.

- BE TRUSTWORTHY.

Trust is a two-way street. If you want to be trusted by people, you must demonstrate that you trust them. You do not need to believe them blindly, but of course, take a calculated risk.

Chapter Six:
Strengthen Connection

A n essential part of reaching a deal is building intimate relations between negotiators. Care to get to know not just the positions on the other side but the individuals you are negotiating with as well. It can be the component that closes the deal to focus on your cooperation.

WORK TOGETHER

A personal connection with the individual or individuals you are negotiating against prevents the agreement from being soured by an antagonistic relationship before it begins. When negotiators see themselves in a conflict as rivals, both sides appear to become protective and reactive to each other. In this case, it is seen as an invasion or an attempt to take control of the other party to ask for even a slight concession. However, it is easier to place these give-and-take agreements in the sense of building consensus if the parties have a close connection. If your opponent thinks you are seeking a mutually beneficial agreement, he or she is much more likely to make a concession.

BUSINESS FOCUS

Keep in mind that business is business. Then there is no need for negotiations if both parties did not have divergent needs. Both sides are going to ask the other to give something up. When you're not careful, this can build a difficult environment. Never commit personal attacks on your opponent's part or attribute any assertive exchange to meanness. Suggest a break when things are getting stressful. It can help you push the discussion back to your relationship by taking time away from the negotiating table. Try not to take anything personally.

RECOGNIZE YOUR OPPONENT

Before they even get to the table, a successful negotiator can develop a personal connection with the entity they will be negotiating against. This means making your opponent make those effective social calls. The key is to frame yourself first as a friend and second as a negotiator, which converts your relationship from rivals to co-operators. This could provide a positive perspective on the individual you are going to be negotiating with. Knowing what they want will help you get whatever you want, too.

MAKE USE OF YOUR NETWORK TO THE FULLEST

Wisely choosing new negotiating counterparts is the most straightforward way of making a negotiation feel secure and trusting.

You will not always choose whom you are negotiating with, but seek referrals and suggestions from those you already trust when you can. Not only are you likely to get some promising leads from others in your network, but if a prospective counterpart realizes that a friend or colleague recommended her, she would possibly treat you right and trust you more than she does if you didn't share a shared bond.

However, be careful not to place all your trust in someone only because she has the seal of approval of a friend.

Dealing exclusively within your network, of course, could lead to missing out on encouraging new opportunities for negotiations.

When reaching out to strangers makes sense, be sure to carefully check their credentials and verify their assertions with independent sources. For instance, Mr. A might neglect to verify the translators' references he consulted in the travel writer's case and relied much more on resumes and first experiences.

BEFORE NEGOTIATING, BUILD RAPPORT.

People appear to react with similar behaviour to the actions of others; research has revealed in the social sciences. We prefer to respond in kind if others collaborate with everyone and treat us with dignity.

We are likely to act that way ourselves if they appear guarded and ambitious. What is more, according to negotiation expert Keith Allred, such exchanges can develop into vicious cycles (those marked by dispute and suspicion) or gentle cycles (those in which collaboration and kindness prevail).

The mutual nature of confidence emphasizes the importance of taking time before negotiating to understand the other side and establish relationships. Until meeting in person, don't presume you can form a relationship simply by swapping a few pleasant e-mails. Rather, by meeting for an unofficial lunch or two, try to forge a deep relationship.

ONLY A FEW MINUTES OF SMALL CONVERSATION WILL GO A LONG WAY.

In her study, Professor Janice Nadler of the Northwestern University School of Law found that negotiators who spend just five minutes chatting on the phone felt more cooperative with their counterparts without addressing issues relevant to the upcoming negotiation, exchanged more information, made fewer threats, and gained more faith in a subsequent e-mail negotiation than did couples of negotiators.

It seems that not only does "schmoozing" and other ways of relationship building create trust, but it can also have a major economic payoff.

SET AN ACCEPTABLE CONFIDENCE DEFAULT.

If you've vetted the negotiating counterpart and spent the time to get to know each other, it would be a mistake to presume that you can trust him instinctively.

Negotiators often wrongly assume a relationship of complete trust with the other party. They are made to feel shocked, hurt, and maybe lighter in the wallet when things go wrong. Bear in mind that even though neither side has acted with malicious deception, negotiators may feel trust has been lost.

Interest conflicts, the common propensity to overclaim credit for one's efforts, and other pervasive cognitive biases may lead us to differently interpret the same events and leap to the wrong conclusion that trust has also been irreparably destroyed.

One method to lessen the odds of trust betrayal is to modify the "trust default" that negotiators hold when conversations begin.

It takes time to address ground rules, such as your core beliefs about trust, as concrete talks begin. Explain that you're just a conservative risk-taker who, over time, would like to build confidence slowly.

For instance, during her first checkup, Carol, the patient in our opening vignette, could have told her doctor that she desires second opinions and seeks to pursue them out when necessary.

You will be able to prevent contention when issues arise by establishing a careful approach to trust from the beginning and keeping your correspondence files and important processes up to date.

WIN THEIR FAITH.

Gaining her confidence is just as critical in developing a mutual trust with another negotiator as measuring how much to trust her.

Start by carefully planning for the negotiation by studying the history, culture, and desires of the other side.

When you negotiate with others from other industrial sectors or countries, this can be extremely crucial. Professor Deepak Malhotra of Harvard Business School told the tale of a technology consulting firm that humiliated itself by being unfamiliar with the word lifts during bid negotiations with an airliner. The airline managers instantly lost faith in the consultants, who would have known with a little advanced analysis that paper tickets in the airline industry are called lifts.

THE LESSON: Take a chance to develop the vocabulary of the other party. You'll encourage the trust and admiration of your counterpart by doing so. Another way to gain confidence in negotiation is to label your most significant concessions clearly, says Malhotra. Remember that most of us instinctively prefer to underestimate the importance of compromises on the other side. To make matters worse, without clarifying how much these "gifts" cost them, negotiators often put concessions on the table.

THE OUTCOME: compromises go unrecognized and unreciprocated, adding to anger, suspicion, and competition. Tell the other party how much you sacrifice but what this sacrifice suggests to you if you make a notable concession, advises Malhotra. For example, when the product supplier received a deferred payment from the restaurant owner for the first time, he should have conveyed that he was only able to accept delayed payment under exceptional circumstances and for a limited period due to his financial commitments.

BUILD CONFIDENCE THROUGH LISTENING AND RECOGNITION.

Allred has found that the more equally negotiators believe they have been handled, the more likely they are to trust and collaborate.

In reality, our expectations of the equality of a negotiating process may have a greater effect than our objective results on our satisfaction level. Be modest about your gains at the table and express admiration for his quick thinking and accomplishments to ensure that your counterpart feels treated equally throughout the negotiation period and reciprocates with confidence.

When you have more leverage than your counterpart, whether you are his boss, for example, or if you have several other negotiating parties to choose from, this can be extremely important. Furthermore, bear in mind that by contrasting her success to that of her colleagues, her rivals, and those who are not at the table, the other party will be able to judge your honesty (and trust or doubt you appropriately).

If this year, you are giving an employee a smaller increase than normal, be sure to tell her that because of belt-tightening in the organization, everyone on her team is facing the same frustrating result.

Finally, allow your counterpart enough time, including any irritation or bad feelings that he might have, to articulate his point of view. Not only can you educate yourself when you listen carefully to others and make an effort to consider his viewpoint, but you will likely help him to feel more secure in you and more optimistic about negotiating in general.

Chapter Seven:
Subtly Influence

I have learned in my experience of teaching negotiating abilities that most people misinterpret the term negotiating. Many people suppose that only in the form of labour/management talks are negotiating skills utilized. I see this differently: in every aspect of our jobs and our personal lives, negotiation and influencing abilities apply. We negotiate endlessly. We negotiate agreements, and what makes relationships run is agreements. We also negotiate to fix issues and to settle disputes we negotiate. If the other party in the negotiation is your boss, subordinate, coworker, spouse, parent, infant, or neighbour, this book intends to support you become such a better interpersonal negotiator. I did not want to remove the word negotiations from the book's title, despite people's misunderstanding of the subject, although negotiating is actually what we need to do. We become less frightened by the word negotiation after we better understand the process. I taught some years ago that more than just negotiation skills were involved in the focus of the class I offered. For the sake of brevity, the word negotiating can be interpreted in this book as combining both negotiating and influencing skills. "A negotiation takes place whenever two or more people communicate, and there is a goal in mind for at least one of those individuals." Negotiation skills are necessary because we spend a lot of time negotiating. Research reveals that most managers and subordinates spend up to 50 percent of their time bargaining. Among others, salespeople, project managers, public servants, engineers, professionals, medical professionals, and people working in the service sector also spend a lot of their time negotiating. In both our work and our personal lives, the results of these negotiations decide our progress. "Or, as Gary Karrass, a noted negotiating skills speaker, says, "In this life, we don't get what we want, we want what we negotiate.

THE SALIENT FEEDBACK

The feedback that is so personally important is salient feedback that makes it far more likely to change our actions. Medical research carried out in Vancouver aims to make the concept behind salient feedback clear.

In this particular study, Group A and Group B were randomly allocated to a group of women. All of them were three months pregnant, which helped maintain that the two groups were statistically equal even before the experiment. An anonymous questionnaire was filled out by all participants in the study about their intake of caffeine and alcohol and their use of illicit drugs without a prescription. On these parameters, before the test, both groups were similar. Then an ultrasound test was given to all participants, after which a technician told every one of them that their baby was growing normally. (The study typically used only women whose babies were growing.) The only difference in the care of the two categories was that the group participants were given the details orally. At the same time, Group B participants were also allowed to look at their babies for 30 seconds on the ultrasound screen.

Three months later, the anonymous questionnaire was again issued to the females in both classes. The experimenters were trying to address the following question: Will it be identical or different for the women in the two groups?

These women had already received a great deal of input during the first trimester of their gestation that things would be different than before. Building a placenta is like climbing the mountain 24 hours a day during the first trimester; hormonal shifts and morning sickness are added to that. This amounts to a considerable amount of feedback that things were dramatically different in these women's lives than they had been before pregnancy. Will it make a difference with 30 seconds of visual feedback? The reply is yes. The mothers who saw their babies decreased their consumption of caffeine, alcohol, and medications dramatically. Why was this visual feedback lasting 30 seconds so powerful? The explanation was that, as the adage goes, "to see is to believe!" ”

Ideas will be recommended in this book to help you get individually relevant input on your negotiation and influencing style to make the concept of salient advice work for everyone.

THE INTELLIGENCE LADDER

The knowledge ladder postulates that four layers of knowledge exist. Knowledge is the first step. We understand intellectually how to execute a certain ability at this level; for instance, we know the difference between being violent and being assertive on an intellectual level. We do not understand how to be assertive in real life, however. At the second level, that is called awareness that comes. We recognize the skill mentally at this stage and know how to do it. We have to learn how to and how not to be assertive, however. You understand how to be assertive about keeping the house cleaner with your spouse, for instance, and you also know that your spouse is having a rough time at work and that now is not the moment to use your assertiveness skills. This is the judgment level. The last degree is that of wisdom. At this stage, you use the right mix of skills with the right people at the right time and in the right context, which considers the history of the relationship, where the relationship is at the moment, and how you'd like it to evolve in the future. The purpose of this book is to apply these principles to the creation of negotiation and influencing skills.

INFORMATION

At this stage, we expand our understanding of the negotiation process and learn about various instruments that may be of interest to us. To explain the negotiation process, we also study a richer and more complex language. We learn more complex concepts, such as "muscle level," "choice points," "value creation," and "value claiming." We learn concepts such as Best Route to a Negotiated Agreement (Fisher &Ury, 1981). (Fisher &Ury, 1981). We may identify various negotiating styles; however, before we acquired this knowledge, we may not be ready to bargain any more effectively than we should have. It's like reading a tennis book: doing so does not necessarily mean that tennis can be played any easier on its own.

KNOWLEDGE

We have built both skills and knowledge at this stage. One begins to be capable not only of identifying the ability in question but to implement the ability. It's one thing, for instance, to be able to explain to a friend what anyone would do to ask an employer for a raise. To be able to negotiate the increase successfully is something completely different. We are all starting to become conscious that we have options about how we respond to such circumstances. This enhanced knowledge and capacity give us comprehension. About how to negotiate, there are several books. Very few combine negotiation skills with the ideals of adult learning if any of them. This book aims to help you better understand how negotiation and influencing skills can be acquired and to provide exercises to promote the learning of these essential skills.

JUDGMENT

Judgment is the willingness at the right time to use the right skills. Learning judgment is partially a method of trial-and-error. By reading about negotiating and watching expert negotiators, we can shorten the time it takes to learn judgment. It would still take some trial-and-error practice for all of us to are becoming more proficient negotiators. This book provides you with a deeper understanding of the value of timing and decision, based on the interviews I conducted with professional negotiators. The book also offers exercises to help you recover from errors as easily as possible and learn what you can from any negotiation encounter.

WISDOM

Wisdom comes from a thorough integration of our data, understanding, and judgment. We are more capable of negotiating good results with experience, negotiating a good mechanism from which these results are derived, and negotiating precedents that we can be confident of.

We need to make better choices about when and how to compromise as we step up the experience ladder. Negotiating can be seen as interactive decision-making, i.e. two or more persons attempting individually and jointly to make the best possible decision on the negotiation result. It makes sense, therefore, to look closely at the decision-making process in negotiations. There are three decision-making styles: non-vigilant, hyper-vigilant, and vigilant.

A non-vigilant option needs to be considered, but we do not see it, or we do not act on it if we see it. As an example, I live in an old Victorian house with my family. I found a slight leak in the back portion of the roof one day, five years ago. It leaked only when the wind from the west was blowing hard, so I missed the leak. It would have cost $600 to patch five years ago. The repair was expected to cost $1,600 last week. I made a non-vigilant decision about repairing my home's roof.

People make non-vigilant choices about driving an old vehicle, which ultimately costs them a lot, or remaining in a friendly relationship long after the friendship has expired. Any of the non-vigilant forms of decisions we can make about negotiating are not to know that we are negotiating, not to take a short break from the negotiation when we need to go into the negotiation unprepared. Hyper-vigilant decisions are at the extreme opposite of non-vigilant actions.

When an individual panics and acts on the first decision he or she thinks of, without considering acceptable alternatives, a hyper-vigilant decision is made. For instance, when it catches fire, a group of patrons are in a film theatre. There is widespread panic, and at the main doors, which are closed by the flames, people stampede. Hundreds of lives are unnecessarily lost because no one turned around to see that behind the movie screen, there were exits. The film patrons took a hyper-vigilant decision because they did not thoroughly consider all their choices.

The sort we want to make more often is a vigilant decision. The best information, analyzed in the best way, is taken into account by diligent decisions to achieve optimum results.

Chapter Eight:
The Art of Persuasion

What comes to your mind when you think of persuasion? Anybody might think about promotional messages that inspire audiences to purchase a certain product. Simultaneously, some would think of a political figure seeking to manipulate the electorate to choose your name on the ballot box. Persuasion is a strong force in daily life has a huge effect on society and the rest of the world. Politics, legal rulings, mass media, news and advertisement are all affected by the power of persuasion and, in essence, affect us.

We also like to think that we are resistant to persuasion. Who we are has a natural opportunity to see past the advertising pitch, consider the facts about a case, and come to conclusions of our own. Perhaps this is true in few situations, but convincing isn't about a strenuous seller attempting to sell you a vehicle or a TV ad that entices you to purchase the new and greatest product

Persuasion can be implicit, and how we react to those influences can depend on several factors. When we think about persuasion, negative references are always the first to come out of the mind, but persuasion should also be seen as a constructive power. Community services campaigns that encourage citizens to recycle or stop smoking are strong examples of persuasion used to change people's lives.

And what's persuasion, exactly? Perloff (2003) said that persuasion would define it as "...a symbolic mechanism in which the communicators are trying to accomplish something by convincing other people to change their perceptions or actions towards a problem by the delivery of a message in a free environment.

HOW DOES PERSUASION HAVE A DIFFERENCE TODAY?

Since then, the art and science of persuasion have been of concern. In the ancient Greeks, there are major variations in how persuasion is taking place now and how it has taken place in the past. In his journal, the Dynamics of Persuasiveness: Contact and Perceptions in the 21st century Century, Richard M. Perloff outlines the five main forms of modernity.

Persuasiveness varies from the past:

The amount of clear messages has risen exponentially. Dream of a moment on how many commercials you see regularly. According to different sources, the number of ads that the average U.S. adult is exposed to per day varies from about 300 to more than 3,000. Persuasive contact flows much quicker. Television, Radio and the Internet all help to transmit clear messages rather easily. Persuasiveness is a big industry and businesses in operation exclusively for convincing reasons (such as advertisement agencies, marketing organizations, public relations companies) and many other companies dependent on persuasion to offer goods and services.

Contemporary convincing is far more subtle than that. Of course, there are a lot of ads that use very obvious persuasion tactics, but often advertisements are much more subtle. For example, companies often deliberately craft very precise photographs designed to inspire audiences to purchase goods or services to achieve their intended lifestyle.

Persuasion is more complex than that. Consumers became more diverse with more diverse choices, but advertisers need to be more sensitive to choosing their persuasive media and post.

The core elements of this concept of persuasion are:

Persuasion is visual, using words, pictures, sounds, etc. It requires a conscious effort to manipulate others. Self-confidence is the secret. People are not forced; instead, they are free to choose.

Methods for communicating clear messages can occur in several ways, including verbally and non-verbally through television, radio, the Internet or face-to-face contact.

PERSUASION TECHNIQUES

The ultimate aim of persuasion is to persuade the target to internalize a convincing statement and take this new mindset as part of their central belief structure. The following are only a couple of the most powerful persuasion Methods. Other approaches include the use of incentives, fines, constructive or negative expertise, among many more.

CREATING A NEED

One form of convincing requires the development of a desire or an appealing Pre-existing needs. This kind of persuasion relates to a person's simple needs for shelter, affection, self-esteem and self-actualization.

Marketers frequently use this tactic for marketing their goods. Remember, for example, how many commercials indicate that people choose to buy a certain product to be content, healthy, loved or appreciated.

CALL FOR SOCIAL NEEDS

Another very successful persuasion tactic is appealing to the desire to be famous, respectable or equivalent to others. Television advertisements include numerous examples of this form of persuasion. Audiences are persuaded to buy products to be like anyone else or be like a well-known celebrity. Television ads are a major source of exposure to persuasion, provided that some figures indicate that the average American watches between 1,500 and 2,000 hours of television a year.

USING WORDS AND PICTURES

Persuasion most often use words and images. Advertisers are well aware of the influence of meaningful terms, which is why there are so many. Advertisers use terms such as "New and Improved" or "All Natural."

GET YOUR FOOT ON THE DOORSTEP

It is another method that is always successful at getting people to cooperate. This kind of persuasion strategy includes convincing a person to respond to a small proposal, such as questioning. They need to buy a small object, accompanied by a much larger order. By getting the individual to consent to a minor initial favour, the claimant already got their "foot on the doorstep," making the person more likely to comply with the broader order. For instance, a neighbour asks you to babysit her child for an hour or two. When you commit to the least demand, then she demands if you should take care of the children for the remainder of the day. Since you have already committed to a specific request, you might feel obligated to consider a larger request as well. This is a really good example of what counsellors and advertisers sometimes refer to as the law of dedication use this approach to enable customers to purchase goods and services.

GO LARGE, THEN LITTLE.

This strategy is the reverse of a foot-to-doorstep approach. A seller will begin by making a big, frequently impractical request. The person reacts by refusing to sell, figuratively shutting the door. The salesperson answers by making a much smaller demand, as is always the case coming off as really conciliatory. People always feel compelled to respond to these deals. Since they rejected the original appeal, citizens sometimes feel obligated to support the salesperson by accepting a small order.

USING THE POWER OF RECIPROCITY

If someone does you a favour, you probably have an almost irresistible responsibility to return the favour in kind. This is regarded as the practice of reciprocity, a social duty to do something for someone else because they did something for you first. I Marketers may make use of this inclination by making it seem like they're doing you good, such as "extras" or discounts, which then push customers to accept the deal and make a purchase.

ESTABLISH AN ANCHOR POINT FOR EVERY NEGOTIATION

The anchoring bias is an implicit cognitive bias that can have a strong effect on negotiations and decisions. In an attempt to conclude, the first bid appears to become a focal point for future negotiation. And if you're looking to discuss a wage rise, you're going to be the first.

The person who offers a number, particularly if that number is a little bit, will help you influence future negotiations. The first number is going to be the starting point. Although you do not get the number, starting high may lead to a higher offer from your boss.

LIMIT YOUR PRESENCE

Psychologist Robert Cialdini is renowned for the six influence concepts he first presented in his best-selling 1984 book Influence: Psychology of Persuasion. One of the main concepts he has defined is known as scarcity or restricting the supply of something. Cialdini implies that when things are scarce or reduced, things become more desirable. People are more likely to purchase anything if they hear that it's the only one or that the deal will soon be over. An artist, for example, could only produce a small run of a single print. Because there are only a few prints left for sale, customers will be more likely to make a buy until they're gone.

SPEND TIME NOTIFYING CONVINCING COMMUNICATIONS

The examples above are only a handful of the numerous methods of convincing mentioned by social psychologists. Look for examples of convincing in your everyday experience. It's an interesting experiment to watch a half-hour of a random television show and notice any convincing advertisement. You might be shocked by the sheer number of effective strategies used in such a short period.

COMMON PERSUASION METHODS FOR PERSONAL USAGE

One of the most common Covert persuasion techniques employed in personal and technical circles is the "Big Picture" understanding. No matter what the situation, the particulars or the primary goal, consider how the target not only remembers their previous encounters but also envision their future. This tactic is especially useful for those who have a goal on the pessimistic side of their case and need to be swayed on the positive side either to win momentum or to close the deal. People are more inclined to be open to persuasion and consider other facts or actions as helpful if they believe the person they are talking to knows them and sees them as an entity (rather than a target). (Rather than a target). Social skills, listening abilities, sympathy and the capacity to translate words and behaviour as an individual's emotional reaction are among those basic human connectivity qualities you are excellent at experiencing while attempting to convince others.

- Listen to the person's experience and history of the subject you're trying to reassure them of.
- Empathize to find common ground to gain their trust and make a personal connection.
- Often ask them where they are and why they feel that way about your subject before attempting some sort of convincing tactic. This is a way to establish a baseline or a starting point to simplify creating a successful persuasion strategy.
- As soon as their position has been defined, ask them how they see the situation or the dispute wrapping up. This lets you know what real future they are searching for and how their dream scenario will end.

Now that you have an understanding of their past and their view of the future (as it applies to your subject), you can select whether more mature, covert or darker persuasive tactics can help you accomplish your ultimate objectives and negotiate into the future that you have dreamed or wished for.

Chapter Nine:
NLP

NLP means neuro-linguistic programming. The aim is to look at a person's neurology, linguistics, and programming to decide better what makes them a special individual. Everyone has their view of reality based on how they were raised and the things they enjoy. When this reality is established, it can become a framework for how various situations are treated. NLP is discussed further in this book, so at this point, you should have a clear understanding of what it entails. When you become aware of how someone else can use NLP tactics for negotiation on you, you will use those tricks on other people.

PHYSIOLOGY MIXING UP

Often switching your physical environment can be the very thing you need to use NLP to reassure or evaluate someone else. There could be something that might obstruct the path throughout the discussion. You may seriously consider moving both you and the individual you're talking to build a friendlier atmosphere. If you feel like the conversation doesn't go where you wanted to, you may want to take a bath break and give the person some space alone. If you're coming back from the bathroom and things are still the same, I recommend that you change the venue. You may want to go for a stroll or venture out onto the balcony. Often you don't even have to go too far. Maybe simply changing your body's movement or the way you're sitting is enough to re-engage the other guy.

VISUALIZATION

Visualization is a perfect way for certain people to meet their targets. There are so many things that may appear out of control, but you'd be shocked how much you can do if you just imagine what you want. It can start by talking about life. Whether you're going to move to L.A., Start dreaming about it to become an actress. Don't tell people you want to do it at some point. In reality, tell me you're going to do it, and you're going to be shocked how much you can influence yourself against these targets. Write it down if you're going to have to. It is more of a form of self-confidence than one that you would do for others, but it also definitely helps to chat and write about the aspirations and desires that you want to see achieved.

TAKE A RIGHT TO SAY NO

We commented lightly on this earlier but take away another human's right to suggest no NLP techniques that can be used for convincing. Instead of asking, "Would you like to go out for dinner tonight? "Ask someone, "Where are we planning to have dinner tonight? "You didn't give them the chance to say no to the date of your dinner. They might say they can't do it anyway, but at least you've been working to take the possibility away. Instead of asking, "Can I have one of them? "Tell me, "How much will I have? "Most people don't even know that you've taken away their right to turn you down.

NEURO-LINGUISTIC PROGRAMMING

Neuro-Linguistic Programming or NLP is a group of methods popularized by the Modern Age and self-help movements for use in communication, self-improvement and behavioural adjustment. The NLP has two functions. You will use it to train your mind to conquer poor habits, to become more creative, and so on. There is no ethical issue with using NLP strategies on your own if you find them useful.

However, the NLP can involve the intentional use of body language, such as replicating (subtly imitating what the other person does, such as piercing your legs as they do) to get someone to like or agree with you, directing or guiding interactions to your benefit, anchoring (using particular phrases to direct other people's thought processes), hiding unconscious hints within sentences or expressions, and attempting to build a rapport to influence them.

Understanding the NLP is important in adversarial circumstances so that you can do so. Defend yourself and respond successfully if you are used by those using the NLP. Some NLP advocates are not happy with conventional discourse and rhetoric skills; they must depend on deception to make their points. Defences include assertively finding out whether someone is against disruptive NLP interrupting you, not authorizing you to respond to questions, shifting a question topic, or purposely attempting to misdirect a discussion. When you're calling someone out with their deviousness, they don't have the edge anymore.

Assertive dialogue can help to protect against NLP strategies. When you believe someone is misdirecting a topic, trying to convince you, invading your room, or driving you into something, you don't like. It's also a smart thing to have solid personal barriers to support.

PROTECT YOURSELF FROM BULLIES AND MANIPULATORS.

The first protection against hidden deception techniques is to understand this. They occur in the first place and are relatively common within Society. Although I do not advocate a pessimistic or optimistic worldview, I do advocate a rational one. Not all are truthful, assertive, or transparent, and often individuals, companies, and governments have their secret agendas to drive forward.

The second line of defense toward covert coercion is to learn all of this. Methods are available in-depth to know and identify if they're still used on you, even if you can see them used by the public. We are supposed to learn about everything, even stuff we don't agree with. Any of the forms covered deception, like propaganda, is more or less one way. You're not engaging with the root of the coercion, so you can also recognize the form it takes.

NLP TECHNIQUE: 'HYPNOTIC TIMING & LEADERSHIP'

This is the origin of hypnotic timing and leading techniques. Essentially, when presenting sensory observations that are completely and verifiably accurate, the unconscious mind would agree with what is said. And you add a point that isn't verifiable; however, you want to be true to your customer because it's easy to obey.

Here is an example of this:

"As you are carrying this book, reading these words, you start going further into a trance." The first two comments are valid, the third major may not be, but it's easy to follow. Having read this and having an understanding of the definition, you are ready to learn more. And that's a good thing because you're going to find out about hypnotic speed and later lead. What I would like to introduce to this stage is an effective NLP technique called a sequence interrupt.

HYPNOTIC TECHNOLOGY: 'NLP SEQUENCE INTERRUPT'

The fundamental premise is that individuals like to adopt a coherent sequence of concepts, feelings and activities. When this pattern is disrupted, an aspect of the mystery is produced that can lead to an immediate hypnotic trance. Some of you may have seen or read handshake induction training used by some NLP coaches, notably Richard Bandler. It functions on the same principles.

Chapter Ten:
Power/Emotion Words

Most negotiations can generate and promote negative emotions because of their existence. Where people meet mainly to further their self-interest or where acrimony has coloured the past relationships of the parties concerned, it is not surprising that feelings are often more influential than the facts in shaping the direction and result of the negotiations. It would be difficult for people to resolve important disagreements without feelings, however. Emotions encourage us to behave and enable us to work hard to overcome differences. When we enable emotion to control the way we negotiate, issues arise. We need to step back and understand the larger picture to negotiate well. To reconcile emotion with reason, we need to be able to interpret the problems and debates rationally. So how do we interact with emotions in a way that allows us to regulate and, where possible, constructively communicate our emotions?

1. Acceptance and Consciousness

To be human is to experience, and in having feelings, there should be nothing wrong. Accept that emotions are natural and normal. Yet, we are also unaware of our feelings. And if we are unsure of what we've been feeling, we are most certainly unaware of others' feelings. Comprehending our own emotions and those of others is the cornerstone of emotional intelligence, the single strongest predictor of success in life. It is necessary to remember that emotions generally come in bundles-some are evident, and some are harder to locate. It is important to become acquainted with the range of emotions that are not quickly discovered, including pain, guilt, anxiety, self-doubt, depression, envy, and loneliness, to tease apart all the feelings we can encounter. We can sometimes suppress or deny our feelings, especially if they are emotions that we don't want to admit to having. Suppression of emotions, particularly strong emotions, typically results in leakage or bursts, however. Often in the most inappropriate way and at the most uncomfortable moment, they will come out. Since our body is closely connected to our feelings, one way to become much more aware of our feelings is to observe how our body behaves. Headaches and achy muscles in the shoulders and neck can suggest panic, a tight chest can signal anxiety, a pounding heart, and transpiration usually signify anger-like feelings, and depression is indicated by exhaustion and slower expression. We will be more conscious of what we are experiencing by studying how our body exposes our inner emotional state. Still, we can more likely discover the emergence of emotional states more easily.

2. How to Handle Intense Emotion

Generally speaking, when a feeling within appears to grow bigger and out of control, identifying or acknowledging the feeling internally can help to minimize the feeling on its own and get it under control. It also helps actually to adopt a detached observer's stance. This helps perspectives to examine feelings and to think about ways to cope with them. It is necessary to remember that even emotional sensitivity and recognition cannot be adequate to regulate actions. Often very intense feelings, such as fear or anger, may lead us to act because of how the human brain works before we have explicitly decided what to do. When we feel rage, much of our blood often goes to our limbs, so while we are well trained for a physical battle, our problem-solving skills would not be at best, to say the very least. Buying more time is always a great way to cope with surging emotions if a person can prevent reacting instantly. Hitting an imaginative stop button or taking a real physical break are some strategies for buying time. Each time you start feeling anxious or when heavy emotions begin to surge, the cognitive pause button can be activated. A trip to the wash-room or a break for brunch or coffee is popular way to take a physical break. The talks may be stopped, and now another meeting or phone call scheduled later if a longer timeframe is needed. It also gives us time to become a distant observer to work out what and why we feel. Be mindful that feelings are not fixed; by negotiating with them, they can be changed. Since our emotions are linked to our thoughts and perceptions, by altering our thoughts and experiences, we can alter our feelings. We may change our emotions by shifting the values and information that lie at heart our thoughts and experiences. It is possible to adjust hot feelings, which are less adaptable and reasonable, to cool emotions, safer and less volatile. Rage, for instance, can be adjusted to frustration and discomfort, depression to disappointment, extreme remorse to disappointment, and anxiety to worry.

3. Emotional Expression

We will determine whether to communicate them until we are completely aware and have adequately identified our emotions. However, there is nothing special about having feelings. It can be dangerous and counterproductive to show them by improper means. When we wish to express our thoughts to the other side, we must properly express them. But don't vent. Just be succinct, carefully describe your emotions and don't blame or judge attributes-just share. Try to connect the tone of emotion to the substantive issue. Build a variety of phrases, from logical conversation to an emotional substance to managing your emotions. Emotions provide both us and the other side with valuable details. Instead of undermining or damaging the negotiating process, if we can convey our feelings positively and at an opportune moment in the negotiation, the negotiation skills would be well beyond average.

4. Emotion, gender and negotiation

Here are some generalizations of the gender gap in negotiation: in many cultures, we are taught that women should not let their emotions to display, particularly while negotiating with men. Emotional displays in business can hurt. A man who raises his voice can be regarded as a tough guy in many cultures who has just lost his cool. At the same time, it's possible to see a lady who raises her voice as someone who cannot control herself. A man who cries can be seen with sympathy (unless it happens too often), whereas a lady who cries can be called "excessively emotional." Typically, these cultural and gender perceptions take a great amount of time to alter. So it's best, particularly when negotiating internationally, to be aware of them.

In your negotiations, how can that translate? We need to compromise on a fair basis in business to achieve and retain the respect we need. For their part, women (and men) may do well before displaying heated emotions to take a little break and leave the room. It is highly valued in business to remain rational at all times during a negotiation, and so letting your head hold control over your heart also at the negotiation table is the way to maintain the respect we merit and have received.

Chapter Eleven:
Stay Results-Focused

FOUR ELEMENTS OF FOCUS

The Ultimate Focus Technique is made up of four primary elements. Here it is:

1. Start. This phase entails an extremely critical phase of finding the right inspiration, choosing the right target and training yourself for the path ahead.

2. Focus. This phase is at the heart of the plan. It addresses that you truly have to devote yourself to a single direction to accomplish your goals.

3. Get intrigued by it. The third phase of the element addresses an important change in your thinking that needs to take place in your daily life to improve the chances of success dramatically.

4. Stick to your goal. The fourth stage emphasizes perseverance and remaining true to the process even though something goes wrong, and you don't appear to conquer all the obstacles. I'm going to discuss each aspect of the plan in a separate section. I will begin each section with a basic overview of the part and then cover it in more depth and answer common scenarios,

concerns, fears and questions that will help you get your head all over the system.

THE PRINCIPLES OF THE FOCUS APPROACH (RECAP)

1. The Focus Approach is a system that consists of four elements and a combination of strategies, methods and techniques to help you accomplish your most critical objectives.

2. There are three situations where you do not need the Supreme Concentration Technique. The first is whether you're close to reaching your goal or having made significant strides. Generally speaking, whether you don't get trapped or if your plan is generally successful, it doesn't make sense to change it.

The second condition is when you're hoping for a wonderful solution to all your concerns. Being focused isn't a fast remedy, and without work on your part, it won't magically transform your life. Be mindful, however, that while the technique can help you remain committed, it will not shorten your path in cases where you need to pay your fees to get what you want, like joining a medical college to become a surgeon.

The last case in which the Overall Focus Plan cannot benefit you is where you lack conviction or trust in your ability. However, that doesn't mean you're never going to reach your goals. It just means that the technique isn't for you yet. Start by establishing some simple, success-friendly values first, and then return to the focused approach after becoming profoundly rooted.

3. The four stages of the focus Strategy are Start, Focus, Get Intrigued and Stick to It.

PHASE 1: BEGIN

The Primary Focus Technique begins by choosing a target or a goal that will become the focal point of your life. You want to pick a few goals as you can because the more goals you seek, the more effort it takes for you to accomplish each target. Pursuing as few targets as possible does not mean that you are not allowed to do anything other than work on them. Having a small concentration ensures that you commit much of your time, resources, and brainpower to as few critical goals as you can. If you have any other objectives, they're going to take a back seat or disappear into the background. You should focus on them while you have spare time, but never to the detriment of your main goal or goal.

Imagine that I was putting an empty glass in front of you and handing you three jars. The first includes sand, the second contains pebbles, and the last contains huge rocks. When you first fill the glass with sand, you're not going to be able to accommodate the pebbles and the large rocks. If you reverse the order and proceed with the big rocks, you're going to fill the jar with no problems.

Big rocks are your most important goals, pebbles are your secondary goals, and sand is everything else that would be good to get, so you wouldn't care if it didn't happen. Limiting yourself to a few objectives as possible, is the primary aspect of the primary Focus Approach, which makes it so successful.

Most methods teach you how to balance your time and resources through various priorities in your life, but they don't believe that a person will be at the peak of their success. In contrast, their resources are split across five or ten different objectives of varying value.

PHASE 2: SACRIFICING IS NECESSARY

Since you need to narrow your attention to as few targets as possible, you will have to give up focusing on other, less important objectives. If you're scared to do so, ask yourself if spacing things has achieved the kind of performance you've tried to achieve. If not, wouldn't it be a fair deal to sacrifice those nice-to-have (but not that important) goals in turn for your ultimate goals?

Let's assume that you're focused on three key goals in your life: saving money to buy your dream home in the countryside, starting to play golf (or any other ability you'd like to master because you love doing it), and working out a six-pack gym (or any other fitness-related goal that isn't necessary for overall well-being). If you determine that owning a dream home is the most important task for you, you may have to agree that— because such substantial items cost so much more money and require time to pursue—you will have to delay learning how to play golf and find different ways to get a leaner stomach. Worse still, you will not be able to accomplish those other goals at all when you're focusing on your main target, so you won't have enough time, resources, or resources to commit to them.

This is the harsh truth about the primary focus Technique that you must accept: you must sacrifice a lot to establish a strong focus, and the more willing you are to compromise, the more concentrated and successful you will be.

However, the sacrifice needs to be clever. You could never neglect important health-related and friendship priorities. When lost, it can be difficult or impossible to restore health and friendships.

STEPS TO GET STARTED

As I was researching this book, one of the most popular questions from readers was, "How do you get started? One of my readers wanted to start a location-independent company that would require him to work from everywhere in the world.

It's a shared goal for many people in today's hyper-connected society where, for many careers, it doesn't matter where you live. Yet, he didn't know where to go. And he has every right to be perplexed; there is so much detail about his target that it's easy to get distracted.

This is only one example of a person trapped in the "Start" stage of the primary focus Strategy. There are even more stories like this—people that have a great urge to get started but are too uncertain as to how to do it. Here are some realistic tips that will allow you to get started:

1. ARE YOU GOING TO HAVE A BETTER STARTING POINT?

There's no need to clarify why the easiest way to get started is to break the target down into little measures and take it from there. However, before we explore how to do it, it's a smart idea to ask whether it would help reach another goal before going on to the goal you currently have in your head.

Notice that this doesn't mean that you have to change your whole strategy—it only means choosing a new starting point to help you accomplish your ultimate target.

For example, while lead climbing is the "purest" type of rock climbing (you bring the rope with you as well clip it to each quickdraw along the way, threatening a relatively long fall), a newbie will do well by learning how to climb the rope first (a simpler way of climbing in which the rope is secured above the path and falls short), practicing simple climbing skills, and then getting started with lead climbing.

It may be tempting to start straight away with the most thrilling method of climbing, but a better and simpler option would be to concentrate on the simpler aim of learning how to climb the rope properly first and then move on to the toughest variation.

If you had to ascend Mount Everest, you wouldn't launch a trip to the Himalayas either. You'd certainly have the ultimate target in your head, but you'd start with simpler expeditions first. If you have no experience in mountaineering, you'd just start climbing in the mountains.

Likewise, if you were to create an eco-friendly, affordable, non-grid house, you wouldn't run to Home Depot immediately to start building the house. You may have set the goal of acquiring basic information about how to build a home, maybe enrolling in a course on eco-friendly house design, assisting with a few tasks, and then—equipped with the right knowledge—begin working on your initial goal of actually constructing your house.

Right now that I'm writing this text, I'm still working on the task of planting a small tree. I didn't start by buying dozens of nursery plants and planting them arbitrarily on a desolate plot of land. I set the goal of first educating myself about forestry, and only then—after equipping myself with appropriate theoretical knowledge—begin the actual journey of planning, planting and helping the forest to grow.

Think carefully about your reference point, and just take it from there until you're confident it's the right first move for you.

2. STRIP IT OFF

If you start with a new objective, you might be puzzled about getting started, particularly when you learn there are a multitude of different approaches you can take. "Disorientation from analysis" follows, and instead of continuing, you get trapped. You don't know how to start.

Whenever I set a new target, I strive to strip it of the most critical piece of guidance, behaviour, habit, or talent required to make it a reality. It's easy to work out the universal thread if you spend a few hours reading posts on the topic or addressing excellent questions to people who understand what you need to know by having made the trip themselves.

For example, if you're new to climbing and start reading posts on how to become a rock climber, you'll soon find that the number one piece of advice (apart from climbing a lot) is to pay close attention to your legs. So there's the first step: go to the climbing gym and concentrate on using your legs instead of your hands as soon as you can. You don't have to learn how to make it happen. Only go bouldering, but you're not using the desire to have a climbing companion as an excuse.

If you want to be a better writer, it's just about reading and writing a lot. You can participate in a writing class, read books on writing, and do all sorts of writing assignments, but to get started, actually writing something—anything—is the ideal route forward.

If you want to develop a company, you can spend a few lifetimes reading business books and studying possible business models. And while there's substance to make sure you chose the best business model for you, if you have little or no experience of entrepreneurship, the first move should be to sell something— anything—just to get a taste of how you can make money on your own.

The goal here is to find out a quick step that you can take right now and do, instead of spending days or weeks struggling to find the most suitable solution. If you take the first move, the energy will cover the rest of you. When you find yourself in need of a policy shift, it would be easier to readjust with the recently acquired knowledge in the real world than if you were already trapped in the philosophy of science.

3. GET YOUR ENCOURAGEMENT

One of the most important reasons people don't get moving on their personal goals is that they don't have social pressure or direction.

When you start studying a foreign language by taking a native speaker class, you can't make an argument because you don't know where to start; just follow your teacher's directions. On the other hand, if you want to work things out on your own, you might easily never proceed because you're frustrated by the amount of experience you need to learn.

If you can't afford to hire an instructor, enter community groups devoted to the goals you want to achieve. It could be a health forum, a business forum, a parenting forum, a travel forum, etc. Don't be scared to ask for guidance, but once you plan to ask for advice, you're able to take steps when a trustworthy forum user answers you, instead of responding with a "yes, but" and a list of reasons.

If you're so fortunate that you have a person who has accomplished the target you want to accomplish in your friend network, have a coffee with all of them and keep asking you how to get started. Once you've issued a series of guidelines, don't question—follow them. There's no need to dilly-dally if you've got a map straight from a guy on the same trip.

Chapter Twelve:
How to Read And Project The Right

THE EYES

O ur eyes are the optical doorway to the universe that surrounds us. From the moment of conception, we are looking for details in familiar faces, gestures or novelty, colour, shading, symmetry, and often aesthetically pleasing. Our visual cortex, broad compared to the rest of the brain, is searching for excitement and new experiences. Our eyes display empathy and kindness, as well as terror and scorn.

Friendly or happy eyes will make a day of ours. But the eyes will still let us know that something is unusual, that there is distress or concern. The Eyes can own a room or a coward in a group of strangers. We adorn our eyes to draw and stop them. Typically, they are the first thing we note about people; that's why when a child is born, we spend so much time staring at the eyes, maybe because we're staring at their souls through the glass.

- PUPIL DILATION—when we're relaxed or like something or somebody we're going to see, our pupils are dilating. We don't have the power of this. When lovers are at home with each other, their pupils dilate while their eyes attempt to drink in as much light as they can. That's why dimly lit restaurants are a nice place to meet because they instinctively soften the eyes and make the pupils bigger—an effect that helps us relax even more in front of others.

- PUPIL CONSTRICTION—our pupils are constricted when we see what we don't want or once we have negative feelings. Pupil constriction is easier to recognize in light-coloured skin. Pupils abruptly diminishing to pinpoints suggest that something negative has just happened. Interestingly, this activity is controlled by our brain to ensure that our eyes are centred in times of pain, since the narrower the opening, the greater the visibility. That's why squinting increases focus.

- RELAXED EYES—open eyes indicate relaxation and trust. When we're at ease, the muscles all around the eyes, the forehead, and the cheek relax—but as soon as we get nervous or anything scares us, they get tight.

Babies also display this very strikingly when their facial muscles unexpectedly scrunch up until they start crying. When attempting to understand any-language actions, often make reference to the eyes for coherence. If the orbits (eye sockets) look happy, the odds are all right. If there is a sudden discomfort from around the eyes or scowling, the person is concentrating or maybe nervous. Eye muscles and underlying tissue respond even more rapidly to stressors than most facial muscles do, giving almost immediate insight into a person's emotional state.

- NARROWING OF EYE SOCKET—when we feel anxious, angry, disturbed, or experienced other negative feelings, the eyes' regions will close because of the underlying muscles' contraction. The brain automatically makes the eye's circles narrower in reaction to fear, worry, or uncertainty. It's a good sign that there's a problem or that something is wrong.

- QUIVERING UNDER EYES—the tiny muscles just under the eyes (the lower portion of the Orbicularis oculi) and above the cheekbones, as well as the underlying tissue, can be very susceptible to tension. Where there is worry, anxiety, or terror, these soft areas will chirp or twitch, exposing the true emotional state of the person.

- BLINK RATE—Blink rates can differ based on the environment and the level of stress or excitement a person is feeling. - Person is different, but the average rate is between 16 and 20 blinks per minute, based on lighting conditions and moisture. People who watch screens blink fewer (many of whom speak of blurry vision or eye infections)

Tears have antibacterial effects, while those operating where there is dust or pollution will blink more. Also, be mindful that wearing contact lenses will increase the number of times we blink. When we're with someone who turns us on, our blink rate appears to rise as well.

- Regular BLINKING—People who are anxious, tense, or depressed will usually blink more than others who are not. Prevalent blinking is mistakenly correlated with deceit. It is only suggestive of stress or other causes noted above since even a simple blink is more common when challenged vigorously.

- EYE CONTACT—eye contact is governed by cultural expectations and personal interests. In some cultures, it is appropriate to stare at someone for 3 to 4 seconds, and in others, anything over 4 seconds is considered disrespectful. Culture also dictates who should look at someone else. Even in the USA, eye contact is dictated by the region of your country of birth.

In New York City, looking at someone for longer than a second and a half may be seen as an insult. Distinct ethnic and cultural communities have their expectations. For example, many African American and Hispanic children are encouraged to look down upon the elderly as a reverence form.

- EYE AVOIDANCE—we do not make eye contact when it's inconvenient to speak to someone or when we deem someone unpleasing, rude, or oppressive. Prisoners, for example, may avoid eye contact with jailers or other prisoners who are perceived to be violent. Avoidance of the eyes can be temporary or long-lasting.

Temporarily, people may turn a blind eye when a person is doing something humiliating. And in the United States, unlike in other regions of the world, when we are in close vicinity, as in the elevator, we prefer to avoid eye contact with strangers even with those we know, particularly if strangers are present. Avoidance of the eyes is not a sign of deceit but may imply guilt or humiliation.

- GAZE SUPERIORITY—Studies worldwide have found that high-level people participate in more eye contact while communicating and listening. Less influential people appear to have more eye contact with all these higher-level individuals when hearing, but less so while chatting. This is also more pronounced in Japan as well as in other Asian Pacific region.

By the way, we seem to prefer people that make direct eye contact with us, particularly if they are of higher status. Eye contact from high social status people, movie stars, for example, makes one feel privileged.

- EYE-CONTACT SEEKING—When we're involved in beginning a chat, whether, in a social or dating settings, we'll aggressively search before we make eye contact that indicates, "I'm here—please talk to me."

- GAZE AND SENTIMENTS—throughout the globe, those who research dating signs have noticed that sometimes the first hint that people's emotions for each other have shifted is how they gaze at one another. Long before words are communicated, the look of increased curiosity telegraphs revealed a significant relationship is moving from polite to more personal.

- GAZE ENGAGING—this is an action meant to get another person's attention warmly or lovingly. What makes this action stand out is the softness of the face and frequent efforts to link, eye-to-eye, with the meekness of the eyes, face, and mouth. This is most often used in dating environments, where it lets the other party feel that you are involved in more contact or proximity. I've seen strangers turn their gazes through large spaces and express their longing.

- GAZING And Staring There's a major difference between gazing at someone and staring at someone. Staring appears to be more impersonal, detached, or argumentative, suggesting that we find someone strange, disturbing, or unusual. On the other hand, gazing is a sign that we find refuge in others, a far more desirable behaviour. When we look, we're on alert; when we look, we're fascinated, even inviting. Staring may offend, particularly in the immediate vicinity, such as a bus or subway.

- CLOSED EYES—at a group, anyone with eyes closed that require time to open or unexpectedly shut and sit longer than normal is likely to have difficulties. It's a blocking action that shows discontent, unease, disbelief, or worry— some type of psychological distress.

  Long pauses in opening the eyes show intense worry. Conversely, in an intimate atmosphere, closed eyes mean, "I trust you, I'm blocking anything else out there, and

  I'm in the present for my other senses." Notably, even blind-born infants can close their eyes when they hear something they don't like or find disturbing.

- EYES CLOSING FOR EMPHASIS—Often, when we try to highlight something or nod incongruence, we're going to close our eyes very briefly. It's a means of affirming what's being said. Like in all actions, context is the secret to ensuring that there is no reflection of conflict.

- COVERING OF EYES—sudden eye covering with a hand or fingers is a blocking action associated with a negative incident, such as the revealing of bad news or threatening content. It also suggests negative feelings, worry, or loss of trust. You see that in people who were caught doing something wrong, too. As I have noted above, congenitally blind children can also do this, but they cannot clarify why; this action has an ancient evolutionary origin.

- EYES CLOSED, RUBBING SURFACE OF NOSE— People who shut their eyes and rub the surface of their nose at almost the same time transmit that they are worried or concerned. This is both a blocking gesture and a pacifier, generally linked with unpleasant thoughts, displeasure, insecurity, worry, or anxiety.

- CRYING—Crying has several private and social functions, in particular comforting emotional relief. Unfortunately, children often understand early that weeping can be used as a manipulative tactic, although some adults do not fail to use it in the same manner. In analyzing an individual's actions, weeping should not be given greater weight than any other indication that a person has a rough time. Crying, whether it happens at a high level, will also help us know that someone is mentally stressed or socially suffering.

- CRYING WHILE GRABBING OBJECTS— People who weep while clinging to their collar, necklace, or shirt necklace are likely to feel more severe negative feelings than a person who just cries.

- EYES DARTING—Eyes that go back and forth tirelessly are typically correlated with the visualization of negative information, uncertainty, apprehension, fear, or worry. Use this action in combination with other details such as facial stress or chin displacement to provide a more precise appraisal. It should be remembered that certain people will turn their eyes back and forth as they evaluate the problem, consider alternatives, or think about solutions. This conduct alone is not, in itself, suggestive of deceit.

- EYE-ACCESSING Sensations- we process our feelings, impulses, or questions. We prefer to look upwards, downwards, or side to side. This is termed as conjugate lateral movement of the eye (CLEM) in the scientific literature. There has been a misconception for decades, well discredited by more than twenty studies that an individual who looks away or side by side when answering a question is deceptive. All we can tell whether someone stares in a certain way when they struggle with a question, or when they answer it, is that they think—not it's in itself reflective of deceit.

- EYELIDS FLUTTERING—Sudden eyelid flickering indicates that something is unusual or that someone is grappling with something (think of the actor Hugh Grant, who often flutters his eyes on-screen when he has issues or has messed something up). People sometimes flicker their eyes as they try to find the right word, or when they can't believe what they've just heard or observed. Disbelief is also seen with a fluttering eyelid.

- EYE POINTING—in certain cultures, the index finger right behind the eye expresses fears or suspicions. But many people around cultures often do this instinctively in the form of a gentle scraping motion as they think or doubt what they say. When you're going overseas, ask locals if this means something unusual. In Romania, I was taught that the finger underneath the eye was a symbol that sometimes means, "Be careful; we don't trust anyone who listens."

- EYE -POINTING CLUSTER—pointing of the index finger just behind the eye combined with brow arching and flattened lips respectively conveys skepticism, bewilderment, or denial. This is particularly valid if the chin is pulled in instead of jutting out.

BODY LANGUAGE

You've got to get straight into their minds to know what they're doing to handle them in the process of negotiation. Master manipulators are eligible for speed reading by verbal and non-verbal cues. When you understand people, you're figuring out the best way to trick them. For instance, certain people are sensitive to emotional reactions and feelings, and emotional manipulation would work better. Similarly, others might be more reasonable by nature. Logical methods of persuasion can work best for these individuals.

You will choose your own body's language, phrases, sounds, acts, and more to influence others before you understand how to think or feel. Here are some of the new insights on knowing the body language of people.

ARMS AND LEGS CROSSED

Crossed hands and legs are a sign of non-verbal resistance. It means that the other guy is emotionally indifferent to what you're worried about, or isn't interested in, or is sure about, what you're doing. They may always have a smile on their faces or speak respectfully. Yet, their non-verbal gestures will paint a different picture of their psychological method of thought.

Crossing arms and legs is a gesture to establish an overt physical or relational separation between the speaker and the audience. When you get a feeling that the person cuts off what you've been doing by crossing their hands and legs, turn the discussion into something important to them. Let the other person be more constructive or open up a little more before returning to the actual topic. The loop continues so consciously or unconsciously that the other person doesn't even know about it.

TRUE SMILE

How do you make a difference between a genuine smile and a false one? This is your lease. Even when we don't seem like we're joking, our lips are still smiling. However, the eyes and the region around the head cannot deceive because it is a very involuntary micro-expression.

It's clear in their eyes that a human is always smiling. A real smile reaches the eye and causes the skin to grow lines or crow legs around the eyes. To hide their true feelings, people are false smiles. Seasoned manipulators, however, can look for crinkles near the area of the eye to determine if the person is genuinely happy or merely a faking pleasure.

EYES NEVER LIE

If people don't hold their eyes for long or remain in touch with their eyes, they will lie to you. When people tell the truth, they maintain the eyes of any single person in their presence. Know if your parents or teachers order you to look into their eyes when they're talking. However, the perception of people who don't look you in the eye has become so common and commonplace that liars and deceivers will now keep their eyes deliberately or purposely too long.

If a person holds his focus constantly, without even looking down slightly, anything of a friend might happen. The easiest way to keep an eye in touch with a human being is to look away at regular intervals.

NODDING IS INCREASED

If an individual nods more than appropriate or nods in an unnecessarily dramatic way, he or she is happy or concerned about your acknowledgment.

This may be used to your advantage when the person is being manipulated. Look out for persons who nod enthusiastically when addressing a crowd. They're the ones that care about you worrying about them. These individuals are subconsciously awaiting your endorsement, making them easy targets for manipulation.

PRESSURE

How does one diagnose emotional stress by the language of a person's body? Clenched teeth, furrowed brows, trembling fingers and stiff necks are among the most common stress signs. We can feel some discomfort, no matter what everybody is doing.

We may not always be sure about the topic or be worried about an issue that specifically triggers their anxieties. If you try to convince them to do something, that's an easy way to catch and play the hero.

Find traces of pressure in people to reach out to them, pose themselves as a method for negotiating, and ultimately convince or use them to do whatever you want! The goal of learning the body language of people is to perceive a clear difference between their words and body language to explain how they think or feel.

NERVOUSNESS

Many nervousness signs involve rapid sweating, fidgeting of the palms, tapping the foot, and high facial expressions. Look closely at how people develop restless legs when they are nervous.

FOOT GESTURE

Guide the foot of a person going while talking to them. The location of their feet, on an unconscious basis, is going to tell something about what they thought. Since the legs are the most ignored or forgotten part of the body, people should not focus too long on the gestures or location of their legs. This makes it an effective way to test implicit thought.

If an individual's feet point to the door or exit, they will run away from the position at the first opportunity possible. However, if a person's feet point in your direction, they're stuck to the chat. When you participate in an interactive dialogue with an individual, your foot will step forward unintentionally. It is taking place at such an unconscious stage that it makes it almost dishonest.

MOVEMENTS OF PUPILS

Our head movements are closely related to various regions of the brain. It exposes the brain's operation that is triggered when you move your eyes in a certain direction. For instance, if you are asked to recall a familiar childhood voice, your eyes would drift subtly up and down to the left to visualize a person or entity emitting a sound. Then, when you begin to recall the tone or the voice, they slowly move downwards, followed by a movement to the right.

The eye movements have a clear pattern (a lot of NLP or Neuron Verbal processing depends on recognizing individuals by their eye movements) based on the brain function involved at a particular time. The brain neurons are intimately associated with our eyes. They activate very split seconds of micro-eye shifts that tell a lot about an individual's thought processes when you're consciously watching them. This is important information for the manipulator while trying to negotiate.

When you ask anyone what they can't remember right now, they're going to turn their head in the way of the upper-left. This means that they are going to retrieve information from memories. Visual learners are widely assumed to rely on their cognitive abilities to retrieve information. Similarly, if a human, when faced with anything, moves his or her eyes to the top left, they don't remember the specifics but instead, make it up. In a nutshell, they do not admit the truth or the memory-answer. They're trying to make myths instead.

When questioned over something, they turn their heads in the upper right direction, and people are more likely, to tell the truth as they attempt to collect facts from their brains before responding. For instance, you're asking a person where they'll be coming from, and he/pointing she's to the top left instead of the top right, he/not she's recalling the truth, but making them up. If it is to affect others, it is important.

If a person struggles with an internal dilemma, he/she will most probably look at their left collarbone. This means that a person is thinking deeply about something or is engaged in an internal debate. For instance, if you ask a man, they will get caught up in a battle between telling the truth and being deceptive.

Similarly, when a person unexpectedly switches his or her eyes from one hand to the other, it is a sign of deception or of seeking some form of escape. They may be terrified to get caught. Quite certainly, the person forms false narratives in his/her brain.

When people remember a particular sensation of physical feeling, their eyes turn to the bottom right. Seek to imagine the satin's numbing sensitivity on your skin when your eyes are closed. The head turns reflexively to the lower right.

ATTRACTIONS

When a person is intensely attracted to you or reflects on a subject with you, their pupil size will eventually increase. Their pupil's contract, whether the discussion topic is boring or the debate, doesn't get them motivated.

People who are attracted to you may also lean in your place or get their feet pointing out to you. Blinking more than just a standard flickering rate is also used as an enticing attribute. When a person blinks more than 8-10 times a minute, they're likely to impress you. These movements occur at a subconscious level as they attempt to control emotions of attraction unconsciously, which is precisely why blinking is linked to flirting in most cultures.

When you impress somebody, their eyes will glow. The explanation behind this is an essential psychological one. When someone is attracted, their eyes would be a little wet. There's light reflecting in it. As a consequence, glittering eyes are a symbol of lust, along with some clues.

PREVENTING MISTAKES WHEN ANALYZING BODY LANGUAGE

Being a master negotiator is about reading people's body language properly when minimizing future errors. You will tailor your responses to their thoughts, preferences, and feelings as you read people closely and persuade them to do what you want. Here are a few strategies when reading body language to identify potential falsities.

ESTABLISH A STANDARD FOR PEOPLE READING

It is important that you read people right to create a blueprint for people's behavior. When you first meet someone, you don't even get a chance to create a baseline. Knowing everything about the temperament or behavior of a human being, though, allows you to get as thorough a knowledge of them as possible from their body language. You're going to get a wider, more reliable and more detailed overview of their attitudes.

Let's say, for example, that an individual is hyperactive, easy to remember, and still awkward to go. He/she is already up to something, and he/she is unable to stay. The subconscious is full of emotions. Now, if you don't learn this basic fact regarding the offender's disposition as a manipulator or observer, you're more likely to misinterpret their body language as fear. Tapping their arms and legs, fidgeting with items, continuously moving their legs, and more may be seen as indicators of nervousness while they can become maybe anxious and want to get things done quickly.

If you have not developed a blueprint for the basic characteristics of this person's disposition, you will end up misunderstanding him or her to conclude that he or she is extremely nervous, not fast-thinking, hyperactive, and enthusiastic.

Before determining their thoughts, feelings and emotions through body language, you need background information about an individual. How does a person normally act or react in different situations, situations or settings? How do they communicate their thoughts and feelings in general?

What is the natural sound of their voice as they run through various emotions? Was there something obvious when they were furious, sad, happy, and excited? What do they express their interest or lack of interest in it? Getting this content should make it easier for you to interpret the person even more effectively and comprehensively in various contexts, thereby reducing errors in people's study. When a pattern of activity doesn't suit their baseline disposition, you can find something off.

CONTEXT

Stop jumping to a conclusion while observing a human, without taking into account the environment or history. For example, a person in the workplace can be very serious and business-like, comfortable, gregarious and relaxed when they see you outdoors. The climate or atmosphere plays a key role in determining the actions of an individual. If you perceive someone outside, you may mistakenly believe that someone is more relaxed and friendly about something that might not be the case. It's also the atmosphere that lets him or her relax.

Past events play a significant role in the assessment of a person. People may simply cross their arms while sitting, and they may feel cold, but not because they are uninterested or suspicious of what you do. In such a case, make them feel more comfortable, or the act of folding their arms and legs will always cause them to move away from what you do on a subconscious level.

Many people learn in the other way, not because they wish to run or are not engaging in conversation, but merely because they are uncomfortable to sit there. Rubbing your nose does not be an indication of lying—it might just be cold, too. That's why you need to look for many tips to come to an almost right conclusion (more on that in the next item).

Similarly, look at a variety of non-verbal signals for a correct interpretation of the person. To understand what they feel or think, consider everything from body language to voice to intonation. If you add visual dialogue or an individual's use of words and phrases for reading, reading is far more powerful.

The mood during a person's reading is extremely critical. You're interviewing a guy for a position first. You should feel nervous since people are usually in a job interview. In such a situation, they cannot hold eye contact or move their hand over their face several times (out of nervousness). This does not automatically mean that they do not tell the truth or have access to deception. It simply means that they are concerned about a job interview in a high-pressure environment.

LOOK FOR A LOT OF TIPS

One of the biggest blunders that individuals make when reading or watching others is identifying signals instead of gazing at them like a swarm. Stop looking for single, stand-alone hints and discovering a variety of clues. For example, if you think of eye contact as a sign of honesty, trust, and authenticity simply because an entity does not have frequent eye contact, you might quickly jump to the conclusion that he or she is a liar.

On the other hand, just when a person has direct eye contact in conversation, you may falsely infer that he or she is a trustworthy person who speaks the truth.

You should ignore all such non-verbal indicators, such as heightened suddenness, twitching legs and hands that continuously touch your chest, to falsely assume that a person is telling the truth merely because he or she has eye contact. To get an accurate reading of a person's thinking habits, thoughts, or sentiments, you need to take a cluster of clues, such as their gestures, body posture, walking, speech, features, and more.

With a single clue, it might be easy to confuse people, but it's almost impossible to replicate all the signals together. The cycle occurs at a very subconscious level, so it is not difficult to focus on faking any aspect in our non-verbal acts to throw off balance on others. So when you're reading a person to persuade them to get what you want them to do, look for many tips that will make you read them more specifically.

CULTURAL INTERPRETATION

Popular are such gestures and expressions, such as smiling, eye contact, and certain other non-verbal signals. They mean the same thing, and they are recognized as having similar connotations across cultures. Besides, there are some movements, acts, and phrases that are interpreted differently across cultures. You can misread the patterns of thought or emotions of another individual based on non-verbal signals within your culture. Have a clear cultural sense for understanding the behaviour of men, so you don't end up staring through your cultural window.

In Italian culture, for instance, people are known to be loud, gregarious and lively in the way they express themselves. Their gestures are passionate and vibrant. They still speak in an angry, sharply pitched tone, marked by exuberant yells and screams. That's the way they show their zeal, their excitement and their affection.

Those non-verbal signs could not be accurately interpreted by someone from Britain or another more muted culture where expectation or passion is more underrated. Once you interpret an individual's verbal and non-verbal speech patterns within a cultural context, it is easier to interpret them correctly.

Also, similar movements can be widely translated through cultures. In western countries, for example, a thumb-up sign can imply affirmation or best regard. However, in certain Middle East parts, the same thumb-up sign is not regarded as a historically recognized expression. It is seen to be unacceptable and insensitive.

Conclusion

Learning to negotiate and influence skills successfully is a lifetime practice.

Negotiation is an agreement in which all sides have a veto on the ultimate result. A voluntary agreement is required on both sides. It is a method of sharing and taking where the exact terms of the contract are decided. That is the act or the negotiating mechanism to achieve a mutually satisfactory consensus or goal. It takes both sides to pass – actual or imagined.

In a very real way, reading this book is just the beginning of the method. To answer the question, "Where am I going from here? "There are a variety of recommendations in this chapter concerning these books. Knowledge is also offered to teach negotiation and operating these strategies in our everyday lives.

Negotiation is a perfect balance for me. I do not want to be a Scrooge, and I sure don't want it to rip people off. I just try to have the best offer available with my businesses and my lines of authority. And I know that if I do not bargain, I'm never going to get the right price. So how are we to cope with this year on year, especially when relationships are rightly considered very important?

During the contract time, one answer for me was to give. An ancient proverb says, 'A gift of man makes room for him.' I don't offer at the bargaining point because, but as we've seen together, it would be perceived as a weakness. And by the way, it can be viewed as a bribe.

I have a client who pays me every month and directs me to conduct public workshops. I wanted to pursue this particular piece of advice, so I only gave him two days free of charge, where I would teach some of his clients and charge zero. It's not a prospecting exercise for me, and it's a true gift to my client with no conditions attached to it. Why are you doing that? I do this because the bond with my customer is the most valuable ingredient, and this is a straightforward way to engage in the relationship at a moment where it cannot be confused in the negotiating process.

Even, if necessary, be willing to walk away. Only make sure you're not bluffing; otherwise, you're going to have to back down. This takes the intestines to exert pressure on the other side to be even more flexible. Negotiations can get very serious. Long hours, conflicting demands, unfulfilled goals, personality and ethnic tensions, and lack of success will frustrate the participants. Tempers rise, angry words are traded, and things may get personal.

The Commandments of Negotiation (In Summary)

1. Still press for more of this. It's a legal tactic to use 'The Shocker' for an opening bid. Don't forget to have good explanations for the opening price. Those explanations must be plausible, and they just seem to be real.

2. Never say yes for the first time and never consider the first counter-offer.

3. Don't succumb to market rot – note, it's the purchaser's job to question all rates. It's up to the vendor to ask for good rates.

Don't ignore that the entire free-market economy is skewed towards a downward effect on prices. The maxim for the buyer and seller is the same: don't succumb.

4. Don't give up at the outset that your position is negotiable. When you use the expression 'It is negotiable' – you have written a blank check to your counterpart. It means you've already given the money up. We can never do it.

5. If the sacrifice is necessary, trade steadily and reluctantly.

6. Never change the price without modifying the proposal. When talking, use the magic expression 'If you... then we...' to make sure that you have a list of all the negotiable factors. Have at your fingertips what can be modified and what the cost to you is.

7. Watch the negotiating operation until the deadline. If you have set the deadline personally, get higher authority to adjust if it is harmful to the negotiation. Often aim to locate timelines or pressure points for your equivalent. Tell them what time pressure they're facing. And use the knowledge to build up your authority.

8. Stop careless or needless harsh words. It can well induce intransigence in your counterparts.

9. Avoid considering rates as the main concern. One of my friends is a senior manager at the largest multinational forklift truck firm. He was accountable for the launch case on one occasion. It secured a substantially lower price from one distributor – particularly compared to other competitors. He pressured the distributor to cut corners, which severely jeopardized the viability of the case. Other expenses that he had to reimburse were borne. He told me that the key lesson for him was to learn to understand when you force a supplier to sacrifice efficiency, merely to ease the price demand. In his terms, 'It's not always a loss to give up on the price.

In truth, the reverse may be valid! 'It is important to note that all factors in and around the contract will be used to boost the deal. The risk for customers is that they try intuitively to offer the seller tunnel a view that shows the price and nothing else.

Well, stop it. Keep looking at all the components of the offer and keep the attention away from the costs.

10. Keep your sense of humour. If you keep going for long and too hard, the thing sours, and one side will leave you saying it was a bad experience. In the end, we're hoping for an understanding.

Lighten the breeze so that it doesn't feel too hot. If you can't express natural laughter in the process, you won't be as successful as you can be.

Lastly, if you have this book on hand, you can quickly turn to a suitable chapter to refresh a forgotten idea or ability. If you don't have a book with you, at least you have a chance to remember a validated method and make a positive impact. Let me remind you of the following acronym: plan and prepare.

References

- Alsadi, A. (2013). *THE SECRET CODES.*

- Bandler, R. (2014). *How to Take Charge of Your Life The User's Guide to NLP* .

- Freeth, P. (2017). *The NLP Trainer Training Manual* .

- Hughes, J. (2014). *Self-Help:.*

- jenkins, G. J. (2013). *The Gentle Art of Persuasion.*

- McRae., B. (1998). *Negotiating and influencing skills: The art of creating and claiming value.*

- Meadows, M. (2017). *The Ultimate Focus Strategy.* Meadows.

- Rate, H. t. (2011). *David Oliver.*

- Seteli, A. (2014). *The Agility Advantage.* Jossey-Bass.

- Volkema, R. J. (2006). *Leverage : How to Get It and How to Keep It in Any.*

- Wodtke, C. (2014). *Radical Focus.*

- Wodtke, C. (2014). *Radical Focus.*

- ZAIDI, S. (2020). *RESULTS: The Art and Science of Getting It Done.*

Printed in Great Britain
by Amazon

12906080R00089